ART OF THE LATE

MIDDLE AGES

Text by HANS H. HOFSTÄTTER

HARRY N. ABRAMS, INC. Publishers NEW YORK

Translated from the German by Robert Erich Wolf

Library of Congress Catalog Card Number: 68-18131

Copyright 1968 in Germany by
HOLLE VERLAG GMBH, BADEN-BADEN
All rights reserved. No part of this book may
be reproduced without the written permission of the publishers
HARRY N. ABRAMS, INCORPORATED, NEW YORK
Printed in West Germany. Bound in the Netherlands

Contents

Introduction   (page 6)

Summary of the Text:

Bibliography   (page 253)

Chronological Tables   (page 254)

Index   (page 260)

Photo credits   (page 264)

Introduction

THE PERIOD. The Late Middle Ages is one of those terms that needs to be defined right from the outset. As with almost all designations that historians use for the various epochs of art, here too the term is no more than a loose but convenient label. From a sociological standpoint, the period began when the city dwellers, the bourgeoisie or burghers, started to play a part in cultural development. It ended with the advent of modern times, when there came about the new humanistic awareness of the nature of man and his world, to which has been given the name Renaissance. The start and finish overlap the preceding and following periods, since every age must perforce develop all of its cultural manifestations out of those which arose long before. With the decline of the earlier Middle Ages, whose society was predominantly feudalistic and whose art was what is called Romanesque, a much vaster part of the population began to make its presence felt at the beginning of the thirteenth century. True enough, the chief institutions of society remained in the hands of the nobility. But among the townsmen and peasantry there began to develop a clearly defined awareness of their identity as a class, and this was encouraged by the fact that they too came to have a share in the chief tasks of their time, both civil and religious. In the cities, artisans and manufacturers acquired economic and political influence. To a very much greater extent than ever before, both city and country dwellers were offered the possibility of improving their lot through education. Even sons of craftsmen and peasants could aspire to high positions and dignities, not only in the Church but now also in the State. The growth of cities and of an economy based on money led gradually but unmistakably to changes in both the material and the cultural ways of life. Virtually symptomatic in this regard was the co-operation of all the social classes in building the cathedrals. Cathedrals were still initiated by ecclesiastics with the encouragement of the royal authority, but very soon the burghers themselves took over and, on their own initiative, carried on the work and completed it. Symptomatic too was the development of the so-called lodges, which were something more than mere workshops, being, rather, the instruments of a new social organization in which all forces united to carry through a single task. It is in this context, then, that the present book considers the development of the Gothic; the question of how the Gothic period gradually liberated itself from earlier bases of thought, and the highly diversified ways in which the Late Romanesque and Early Gothic overlapped, are subjects treated in the volume on the Early Middle Ages in this same series.

In the works of art pictured in this book, no attempt has been made to follow a strict chronological order. Rather, the aim has been to show the many-sided interpenetration of a great many means of expression and to point out the problems connected with the development of various themes and subjects which maintained their continuity despite all the historical changes in style. If the result gives the impression of a kaleidoscope rather than a methodical presentation, it is because the living development of art does not obey abstract schemes. Art follows organic laws of growth, dipping backward in time or plunging ahead into the future, often turning up with what seem to be very similar solutions in completely different periods or in widely separated geographical situations. The participation of all social classes in late-medieval culture and the constantly renewed influx of new impulses from the folk themselves, which either clashed or blended with the traditional aristocratic notions of art, created a picture of the greatest diversity, and over and over again they opened up new horizons of the utmost historical significance. This introduction can do no more, therefore, than call attention to the most meaningful aspects of the art of a period which stretched across three centuries.

ARCHITECTURE. Religious architecture in the Gothic period was more than a matter of building churches. It was nothing more nor less than the leader of all the other arts, and not only because all the arts had their place within a church and were therefore related in function to architecture. Even more, its leadership is proved by the fact that the sculptor installed his statues in architectonic settings, that the goldsmith designed his reliquaries and monstrances in architectonic forms, and that painters so often depicted Gothic buildings in their pictures and, what is more, set their pictures into elaborate frames which resembled architectural structures. In the thought of the time, the Gothic church had a significance beyond the fact that it was the place where the faithful came to participate in the Mass and to listen to the sermon: it was, quite literally, intended as an image—and not only as a symbol—of Heaven itself. The development of this notion actually precedes the period of the building of the great cathedrals. It was first propounded as a consistent idea by Suger, who had been abbot of the monastery of Saint-Denis near Paris since 1122. As builders gained increasing mastery of the technique of vaulting, churches took on the form of a heavenly city, an embodiment of the apocalyptic vision of the Heavenly Jerusalem as set down by Saint John the Divine in his Revelation. As regards its design, the prototype of this conception is to be found in Antique Roman civil architecture as we know it from the palace

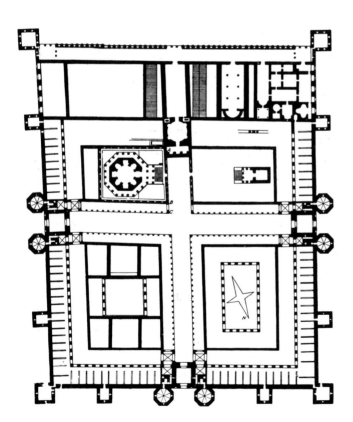

Ground plan, Palace of Diocletian, Split, Yugoslavia. c. A.D. 300

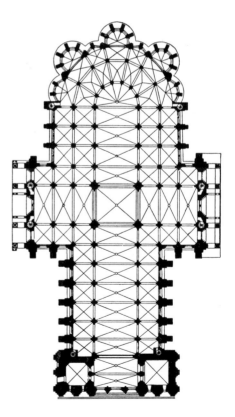

Ground plan, Chartres Cathedral

of Diocletian which still stands in the Yugoslavian city of Split. A wall protected by battlements and watchtowers encloses a city area whose ground plan is organized around two great principal streets which form a cross. From the main gate a long arcaded street leads to the audience chambers of the ruler. The great street which crosses the main street is similarly arcaded and connects the two side gates. The general plan of a great cathedral is very similar to this. Like a city walled about with battlements and watchtowers, whose gates are guarded by angels, prophets, and saints, in the interior there is a long arcaded street whose open sky is replaced by cross vaults which, in fact, were usually painted blue with gold stars. The main street is crossed by another, the transept, and leads to the throne room of the Eucharist, the choir. According to John's vision on Patmos, this city must be imagined as soaring in the air, with walls not of solid stuff but of precious gems which cast their own light. Such an impression of soaring, as our pictures will show, was achieved in Gothic architecture by holding in balanced suspension those lines of force which strain upward and the opposite lines which bear downward, with the result that the entire structure appears to be reduced to no more than those essential lines of force. The effect of walls of glowing gems was achieved by reducing the stone walls to a minimum and replacing them with large, varicolored stained-glass windows, whose thousands of pictures of sacred events were intended less as pictures to be looked at than as the medium through which the sunlight streaming into the church acquires its transcendental character. The notion of the Heavenly Jerusalem perhaps appears again in the great circular windows which rise above the portals. Along with their complex symbolism as the Sun (Christ) and the Rose (Mary), medieval commentators on the Apocalypse held that they were to be understood, along with the rows of arches below, as the sign of the round city that exists in Heaven. In this there were also allusions to Oriental notions of the ideal round city which, in fact, had been realized at least once, in the old town of Baghdad.

The eye can scarcely take in all the wealth of figurative decoration that was lavished on a cathedral. The entire range of theological and secular knowledge of the time was given visual form, not just to be looked at but, even more, simply because it was thought to belong there by right. Superabundant as are the many kinds of images to be seen in a cathedral, they nevertheless follow a basic plan of organization, although the plan was subject to some variation without affecting its general validity. Generally the decoration of the west entrance, the main portal, concerned the Last Judgment and the weighing of souls. This theme appeared above the principal entry into the City of Heaven as a symbol of the choice men must make between good and evil. The two side portals, fronting the transepts, are related to each other in subject matter, one representing the Old Testament, the other the New. The shady, cool, sunless north portal has figures of the Old Testament prophets, sibyls, and patriarchs, and they are grouped around Mary who, as Mother of God, created the bridge between the old and the new covenants. Usually the rose window above this portal also reflects that idea. The sun-drenched south portal is under the aegis of Christ, whose statue appears on the central doorpost and is flanked by Apostles, martyrs, and confessors. As a rule, the "sun window" above this portal shows Christ enthroned as King of Heaven.

The idea of the church building as the Heavenly Jerusalem was not a creation of the Gothic. The notion had appeared much earlier in the liturgy. Thus, the prayers prescribed for the laying of a cornerstone declare that what is being begun is not a building but the city of which St. John wrote, in the Revelation, that he "saw no temple therein: for the Lord God Almighty and the Lamb are the temple of it." But it was the Gothic that first discovered the means to embody this vision in stone. Decisive for this was the system of vaulting which developed out of Norman architecture, above all the exploitation of the cross-ribbed vault for structural ends. In Romanesque architecture the heavy vaulted domes bore down, with all their massive weight, on the entire span of the walls of the nave. The walls themselves therefore had to be strengthened by reinforcing walls and arches, and, to make use of all the space possible, the walls were hollowed out to form galleries. The Gothic, however, discovered how to channel the thrust and weight of vaulting into stone cross-ribbing so that they would be displaced onto the four impost points of the ribbing. At those four points the thrust is transformed into a perpendicular force which is transmitted directly downward, so as to be borne by the piers of the arches. At the same time, the sideward thrust of the vaulting is carried off to the buttress piers which run around the exterior of the building. Thus, from the standpoint of construction, all that matters are the four corner points of each unit of vaulting, that is, of each bay. Once these are reinforced in the same manner, the walls that lie between them are no longer of structural importance. They can be reduced to a minimum by substituting large windows for their solid stone surfaces or by breaking them up with rows of arches. In this way, the wall itself becomes transparent, open to light and air, and virtually diaphanous. Since, in this system, the succession of vaults in the longitudinal axis of the church is likewise held in equilibrium, and no longer needs to be propped up by massive interior structures functioning as abutments, the interior of the church can be laid out in a much more unified design than was possible in Romanesque architecture; and this meant that the entire interior could be conceived differently from in the past. Basically the same plan was perpetuated, the basilica design, but it was modified to create a higher and better-illuminated nave between much lower side aisles. The builders of the classical cathedrals in France, in their determination to unify completely the whole interior, rejected all structural components which stood out as isolated units, in particular the crossing tower and the crypt. In so doing, they made it appear that the roof vaulting of the nave and choir was, like the ground level, part of the regular rhythmic progression governing the total internal area of the church. The diffusion of this Gothic architecture to every corner of Europe, and the variations and reinterpretations which it underwent as it met up with native and local traditions of building, constitute one of the most dramatic chapters in the cultural history of the Western world.

SCULPTURE. The function of medieval sculpture was to give visual form to the things of religion. Compared with the preceding Early and High Romanesque periods, the Gothic employed a greatly expanded repertory of images. It was no longer confined to subjects drawn directly from Scripture, and the entire body of secular knowledge of the time was brought into relationship with the divine plan of salvation. A cathedral, with its sculptural decoration and stained-glass windows, became a virtual encyclopedia in images. Not only were the personages of the Old and New Testaments portrayed, but also the parables of Christ, the seven works of mercy, the seven liberal arts, the zodiac with all the activities of men appropriate to the seasons and months, and even historical events. There were contemporary references too: living ecclesiastical or civil patrons of the church might be portrayed in stone, and in French cathedrals there was often a royal gallery on which portraits of all the French monarchs since Charlemagne symbolized the imperial tradition, as an open challenge to the rival claims of the German imperial dynasty of the Hohenstaufens.

The fourteenth century, a period of profound mysticism, added no new themes to this repertory of images. Its changed religious attitude was opposed to the elaborate schemata of all knowledge that the Scholastics had devised in the twelfth and thirteenth centuries. Instead, the new character of personal devotions fixed the attention on single incidents which were isolated out of the great body of religious imagery and set before the eyes of the believer as separate statues or pictures. Thus various types of devotional image were singled out for special treatment: statues of the Madonna, crucifixes, represen-

Cross section of the basilica-plan nave, Chartres Cathedral

Elevation of the nave, Chartres Cathedral

tations of Christ's Passion, the *Pietà*. These were conceived independently of any predetermined location in which they were to be shown, and unlike cathedral sculpture were not related to the environment as such but only to the private meditations of the believer. They could be set up in churches or chapels, but also in the domestic quarters of a family. Their small format tells us that, for the most part, they were meant for private devotions, not for veneration by entire congregations.

The narrowing of subject matter that mysticism brought with it was succeeded, in the fifteenth century, by a new insistence that images should be large enough to be seen easily by the multitude, though works of art remained independent rather than part of extensive cycles as had formerly been the case in cathedrals. As a result, a new element was especially stressed: altarpieces were constructed with side wings which could be changed according to the liturgical cycle of feasts. Their construction followed the rigorous rule of changeable and fixed parts, exactly as in the Mass itself in which some texts are always recited, others changing according to the day or feast. Generally the predella remained fixed, as did the framework rising above the altarpiece. The altarpiece itself, however, could be changed to suit the occasion, as in Grünewald's Isenheim Altarpiece, which can be opened to show three different views; and in some cases the predella likewise was movable. Such Late Gothic transformable altarpieces can be thought of as miniature cathedrals insofar as they may involve all the various mediums of art: architecture in the over-all construction and in the altarpiece itself, sculpture in the carvings, painting in the movable wings and predella, in which latter there can also be sculpture.

In Gothic sculpture there was an increasingly urgent desire to represent men themselves, not merely

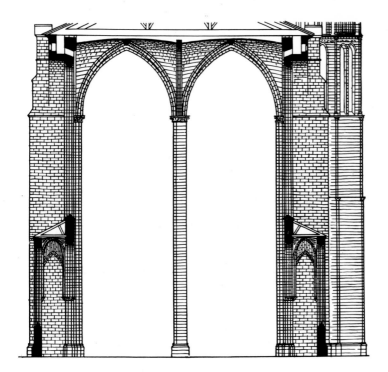

Cross section of the hall church of the Jacobins, Toulouse

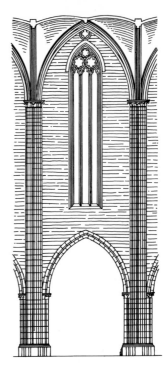

Elevation of a bay, church of the Jacobins, Toulouse

symbolically but also as they truly looked, and wished to look, as individuals. Initially, tomb sculpture had characterized the deceased only in terms of his station in life—a bishop, abbot, or knight. But from the thirteenth to the fifteenth century one can observe a steadily increasing effort to depict the actual appearance of an individual. Over and beyond those particular commissions in which the sculptor was personally acquainted with the patron he was engaged to portray, from the thirteenth century on it was more and more expected of a sculptor that he should portray men in all their humanity. In French art, even in portraits of kings, individual human traits were subordinated to rigorous norms of abstraction. But in German art, to a much greater extent and much earlier in date, the desire to reveal the inner character of human beings broke through the severe rules which had long been in force. This occurred for the first time in the south portal of Strasbourg Cathedral, then in the choir screen at Bamberg, and then in the work of the Naumburg Master especially. To be sure, none of these are literal records of what certain individuals looked like. Instead, they intensify human characteristics to a point where what results truly deserves the name of portraiture. In this the Naumburg Master had no successors. After him, once again the idealized image prevailed. The French statuette of Saint Louis with his consort (page 111) does portray the King with some accuracy, but individual features are nevertheless subordinated to the ideal concept of sovereignty which the age held. Around the middle of the fourteenth century, Peter Parler restored to portraiture the spiritual and corporeal force which, before him, only the Naumburg Master had been able to achieve, although in the case of Parler he was specifically commissioned to do busts which were intended as portraits. But once again no one carried on this advance, until a new impulse came—this time from Flemish painting—in which men's spiritual essence was pinned down in the unique, unmistakably personal traits of human individuality. Beginning with Nicolaus Gerhaerts, there was a steady stream of portraitlike statues, some of them real likenesses of architects and sculptors, others—such as the Apostles on the carved altarpieces of a Riemenschneider or a Veit Stoss—once again, not real portraiture but embodiments of human qualities intensified into artistic expression. When this occurred, the inheritance of the Naumburg Master was taken up again, and, in Germany, it led finally to an acceptance of the humanism of the Renaissance.

PAINTING. With the end of the thirteenth century and the beginning of the fourteenth, painting freed itself from the bonds which, in the Early and High Middle Ages, had traditionally made it the servant of manuscript illumination and mural art. For the first time, with Giotto, a picture was created as an independent entity, complete in itself, its composition based on a unified pictorial space in which a single incident taking place in a specific time was presented in such a way as to direct the viewer's eye to a particular point. Although these innovations were largely neglected by Giotto's successors, little by little they began to implant themselves in all the traditional practices of art. This, however, was more true of Italy than of the lands north of the Alps. But even in the North, mainly through the exchange of artists and works of art between the court circles of Paris, Avignon, Dijon, and Prague, the new ways of seeing and thinking brought about a steadily progressive change. Little by little, landscape came to be understood as a spatial continuum such as men knew from their own experience. Perspective brought pictorial space much more into line with the real space men lived in, and thereby the viewer became more truly a spectator or even a participant in the events depicted. Painted figures acquired a new corporeal volume which made them appear to be real figures taking up room in a real space. A thing, an object, was comprehended as something material to be represented by the painter's means in such a way that the viewer could immediately identify what he saw as metal, cloth, fur, gems, and the like. Observation of real things filled the painter with a passionate concern which is particularly evident in precisely those pictures in which this new way of seeing had not completely ousted the traditional conceptions, so that both are present, uncomfortably, side by side. The Netherlanders were more preoccupied than the Italians with the representation of real things and their subordination to an over-all conception. That explains why the Netherlanders also created the first portraits in Western art to be true to life. They began by observing individual traits which they brought into relationship with the spiritual character of the person portrayed, at first in a manner rather like a still-life arrangement, but ultimately by linking everything with the movements and character traits they observed. Even religious art was profoundly affected by the newly discovered reality and exploited it to speak to the men of the time with extraordinary intimacy and the conviction that familiarity brings. The introduction of perspective meant that there was no longer a chasm between the sacred and the profane. Scenes which before had seemed unreal because of their gold backgrounds now were presented in landscape settings which offered yet another proof of the glory of God's creation.

When one looks at the development of art in all its many forms, one can scarcely make out, in the Late Middle Ages, those traits of disintegration and decline that writers in the past claimed to see in a period whose ideas they thought visionary and whose art they deprecated as primitive compared with that of the Renaissance and its reawakening of the ideals of Antiquity. In the light of the history of art, the opposite is true. It was a richly creative age which invented or adumbrated artistic conceptions that not only expressed the bond between man and the world in a way satisfactory to its own time, but which also proved itself significant and rich in consequences for the centuries that came after it.

The rose window of the north transept, cathedral of Notre-Dame, Paris. Built by Jean de Chelles shortly after 1250 (the glass dates from c. 1255). Diameter 42′4″. In the center, Mary enthroned with the Christ child in her arms, surrounded by successive circles with Old Testament Prophets, Judges, and Kings in medallions radiating out from the center

13

Cathedral of Notre-Dame, Chartres, rising above the roofs of the city, on a hill which was already a place of worship in pre-Christian times. Substantially complete by 1260

Portal and window zones, west façade, Chartres Cathedral. Begun c. 1145, the façade was completed by the rose window in 1210–20 ▶

The classical Gothic epoch begins in France with the cathedral of Chartres. In the façade can be seen the conflict between the old Romanesque tradition and the new Gothic conception. The original plan of a recessed portal was abandoned around 1150, and the portal was then laid out on the same frontal plane as the towers. There are still marked horizontal separations between the stories, and the windows are still set in Romanesque semicircular arches, though already the middle window is raised higher, according to Gothic tendency. Nevertheless, the old Romanesque plan of a solid exterior wall has been superseded, and the interior has been opened up to light.

At the left can be seen how bridgelike arches, whose lower radii are smaller than those above, displace the outward thrust of the vaulting to external piers. In the interior, it is still only the downward push which is compensated.

In the interior of Chartres Cathedral the decisive innovations of the Gothic appeared for the first time, though even there they had not yet fully triumphed over the Romanesque tradition. For the first time the system of galleries is abandoned and the walls are reduced to three stories in perfect equilibrium. Over the ground-floor arcades, whose piers still recall the earlier system of alternating support, runs a horizontal arcaded gallery, the so-called triforium. Above it rises a story composed of pairs of tall windows, another decisive innovation at Chartres. These fill the entire available area of the wall and extend far above the beginnings of the vaulting. Immediately above each pair, a round window extends right up to the vault. Thanks to support from the abutment piers on the exterior, the walls could be made into an open latticework of windows, and to this is due the impression that the entire interior space seems to soar upward.

Old Testament figures on the north porch, Chartres ▶
Cathedral. c. 1217

◀ *Christ Blessing*, statue on the *trumeau*, south porch,
Chartres Cathedral. c. 1217

In contrast to the south porch, the north porch at Chartres is devoted to the representatives of the Old Testament. On the *trumeau* stands Saint Anne with the infant Mary in her arms. On the left wall below her appears the group of figures on the facing page, depicting, from left to right, Melchizedek with chalice and censer, Abraham with Isaac whose hands and feet are bound in readiness for the sacrifice, Moses with the Tablets of the Law, Samuel with the sacrificial lamb, and King David with spear and crown. The David is the latest in date of the figures and the most sensitively conceived.

Christ (left) holds in one hand the Book of Life, and His other hand is raised in benediction. Beneath His feet are a lion and a dragon, the one possibly a symbol of the power of the *Logos*, of God's Word, the other representing evil overcome. The figure is rigorously frontal. Viewed straight on, it gives the impression of being a solid block. However, this unusual oblique view brings out, in dramatic fashion, the tense strain between an organic feeling for life and the eternal immutability of the stone in which the statue is carved. On the jambs, Apostles, martyrs, and saints surround the figure of Christ.

Statues on the portals of cathedrals are not mere added decoration but form an inseparable unity with the structure itself. Without them, the significance of the cathedral as an image of Heaven and of the ecclesiastical hierarchy could scarcely be expressed. The figured portal developed out of the Romanesque portal which was flanked by columns, and indeed the figures are themselves columns on which, symbolically, the spiritual structure of the Church reposes. Without involving any change in this basic concept, such statues became increasingly independent of their structural function, as well as more individualized. At Chartres, this relationship to architecture is particularly clear. Each figure is differentiated by its over-all pose, but at the same time there are subtle correspondences in the positions of the hands or in the flow of draperies, and these carry over from one figure to the next to tie the entire group into an architectonic unity.

Saint Theodore, on left jamb of left portal, ▶
south front, Chartres Cathedral. Between
1224 and 1250

These two figures from portals on
opposite sides of the cathedral not
only differ from each other in expressive character but also make
clear the development which took
place in sculpture. In pose and expression the figure of the Baptist can
be called mannerist, a visual embodiment of asceticism, of submission to
the saintly duty and mission. In contrast, the Saint Theodore is the ideal
image of a Christian knight. His
bearing is not something imposed on
him from outside but is the product
of his own self-determination: he is
where he is in the procession of
figures on the portal out of his own
choice. His feet bear the entire
weight of the body, the figure is conceived almost as a freestanding
statue, and the gaze and bearing
speak of fixity of purpose and self-
confidence.

◀ *John the Baptist*, on right jamb of central
portal, north front, Chartres Cathedral.
c. 1200–1210

Here we have the first use of stained glass to make a tympanum over the central portal, and the triforium is likewise glassed in. The large rose window, which is capped by a glass spandrel above, to form a Gothic pointed arch, was completed in 1285.

West façade, Reims Cathedral

The portal was built 1236–52, completed 1250–60. Between 1255 and 1290, the façade was erected to above the level of the rose window, and the main features of the general structure were completed by 1311. The north tower was finished in its present form in 1427.

In the harmonious blending of all its elements, Reims Cathedral surpasses all other French Gothic constructions, even Chartres, to which it owes so much. Already in the façade a fundamental conception of cathedral architecture is clearly expressed; the idea of the House of God as a simulacrum on earth of a celestial prototype. This impression is not mere fancy: the façade literally soars aloft. Its horizontal and vertical planes interpenetrate in such a way as not merely to support each other but also to intensify, to heighten, one another. Furthermore, the separate stories interlock in a manner which makes it seem as if each new story grows organically out of the one below. Only the lowest zone of the ground floor is precisely defined as a structure firmly planted on the earth. Above it, the exact point at which the rose window begins is concealed by the steep gables of the portals, and the same occurs with the towers, whose bases are covered by the royal gallery.

The nave at Reims adopts the same three-storied articulation as Chartres, but welds the divisions into a firmer unity. The system of alternating supports is no longer used here, and instead there are round piers with engaged colonettes, the whole bound together by a single capital. At Chartres the tall windows were still composed of three parts—two lancet windows with acute arches plus a round window. Here they are combined into a two-part window in which, for the first time, the upper part is made up of bar tracery, a motif destined to be of great importance in the future development of architectonic decoration. The interior façade of the west wall is now also conceived in terms of space. It not only allows for more intense illumination but, also, is broken up into a great number of niches, each of which holds a statue. Here too one feels how the vault soars upward above its steeply vertical supports.

Chevet, Reims Cathedral, largely completed ▶
by c. 1241

◀ View of the vaulting over the choir, Reims
Cathedral

Reims Cathedral displays (facing page) the most elaborate system of flying buttresses devised up to that time. To help bridge over the wide area between the ambulatory and the apsidal chapels, a central supporting pier had to be added. The windows show how stonework tracery developed out of the combination into a single unit of the three separate windows such as were still to be seen at Chartres.

Clearly recognizable (left) is the system of cross-rib vaulting at Reims. In the choir it intersects the longitudinal axis diagonally, whereas in the polygonal apse, which rounds out the choir, it spreads out fanwise. The intersecting ribs bear the entire weight of the segment of vault lying between them and carry it off to the side walls, discharging the downward pressure onto the so-called responds—the engaged columns of the piers—and the arcades of the nave. At the same time, the outward thrust is diverted to the exterior system of the buttresses. A single section of the interior which is roofed over by a cross-ribbed vault constitutes a bay, and the interior space of the cathedral is unified by a succession of such bays.

The system of buttresses, as used in Reims Cathedral, is a decisive architectonic motif which, at the same time, has symbolic significance. A small, high tower crowns each pier, and beneath its spire is a baldachin set on pillars, under which stands a statue of an angel. This motif is used also on the buttress piers of the long sides and carries over onto the façade itself. What results is something like a many-towered City of God whose walls are guarded by angel-sentries. In the apse, this symbolic character is accentuated by gargoyles perching on a balustrade, and behind them the high choir rises like a citadel. Yet, however much the church may resemble a symbolic fortress, as architecture it remains seemingly weightless, transparent as glass because of the great number of broken-up surfaces and prismatic pinnacles.

The anonymous master who created this Visitation ranks among the most important sculptors of the Middle Ages. In comparison with the wall statues of Chartres (page 19), it is evident that, by this time, sculpture had gained great freedom with respect to its architectural setting. These statues stand in front of the columns, in a space broadly delimited by the pedestals below and the baldachins above. There can be no doubt that the sculptor was acquainted with the art of Antiquity, and that he put that example to good use in the new Gothic feeling for the human body. This is shown by the way he treated the fine folds of the drapery which cling to the body contours, and also by something approaching classical *contrapposto* in the poses, that is, the concentration of the body weight on one firmly planted leg while the other leg is free of weight and is poised lightly to one side. The folds of the drapery are used to outline the volumes of the figure, following closely its lines. What is more, the anonymous master interpreted the meaning of the Visitation with great sensitivity. The two women, each embodying her own separate world, meet in a dramatic relationship in which they are both linked and isolated. Mary's face is youthful, almost Roman in its idealized grace, with harmoniously balanced proportions. Elizabeth's, by contrast, is more generalized, the face of an elderly woman of age-old wisdom—the face of a sibyl.

Originally intended as a figure attendant on Saint Nicasius, the expressive significance of the statue led to its being transferred to a more central position in the portal of Reims Cathedral.

The smiling angel as bearer of good tidings is one of the most successful innovations of the master sculptor at Reims. What he attempted was not a psychological conception. Instead, by exploiting the plastic possibilities of the physiognomy, he sought to give visual embodiment to the notion of "joy." As a consequence of the new, subtle understanding of how all parts of the human body work together functionally, the sculptor made of this smile something unforgettable.

The conception of the inner façade of the west end of Reims Cathedral had neither precedent nor succession, a unique artistic achievement. Earlier (page 23) we saw that part of the west wall that is visible from the nave. Here we have a detail from its lowest zone. The entire wall is covered with trefoil-arched niches, each containing a statue. Each tier of figures is separated from the next by an ornamental framework with a luxuriant growth of plants in low relief. The flatness of the exterior surface contrasts with, and emphasizes, the seemingly indeterminate depth of the niches themselves. Here, in a way completely novel for the Gothic, the relationship between figures and space is unified: each figure fits into its own clearly marked-off area, so that the surrounding space becomes an inseparable component of the figure itself. Giotto devised something similar in the painted niches of the Scrovegni Chapel in Padua, thereby posing for the first time one of the basic problems in Occidental painting of the modern era, the problem of the pictorial representation of figures in space.

Figures in niches on the inner west wall, Reims Cathedral, possibly depicting the encounter of Abraham with the priest-king Melchizedek. Third quarter of thirteenth century

The medieval cathedral was not only a metaphorical image of Heaven. It also embodied the religious reality of the Middle Ages in the form of images which, together, make up a Scholastic encyclopedia. In the systematic philosophy of Scholasticism, thought is subordinated to the sacred obligations of faith: the aim of intellectual activity is to understand the already existing, God-given truth, and to set it down in theorems and conclusions. Thus, everything man can think and know was depicted in the cathedral, as a visual reminder to the unlettered laity of what they had been told in the sermon, but also, and above all, as a positive demonstration of the reality of God, since everything which can be depicted must exist, otherwise it would defy depiction. And so, here, along with the sacred personages of both Testaments, the legends of the martyrs, the personifications of Virtues, Vices, and the Works of Mercy, there are also the sciences, the arts, the activities of men appropriate to each season, the entire cosmogony of the medieval world-picture.

Quatrefoils with the signs of the zodiac Libra and Scorpio, and below them the characteristic labors of the months. West front, Amiens Cathedral. c. 1220–36

View of the right jamb of ▶ the central portal, west front, Amiens Cathedral. c. 1230

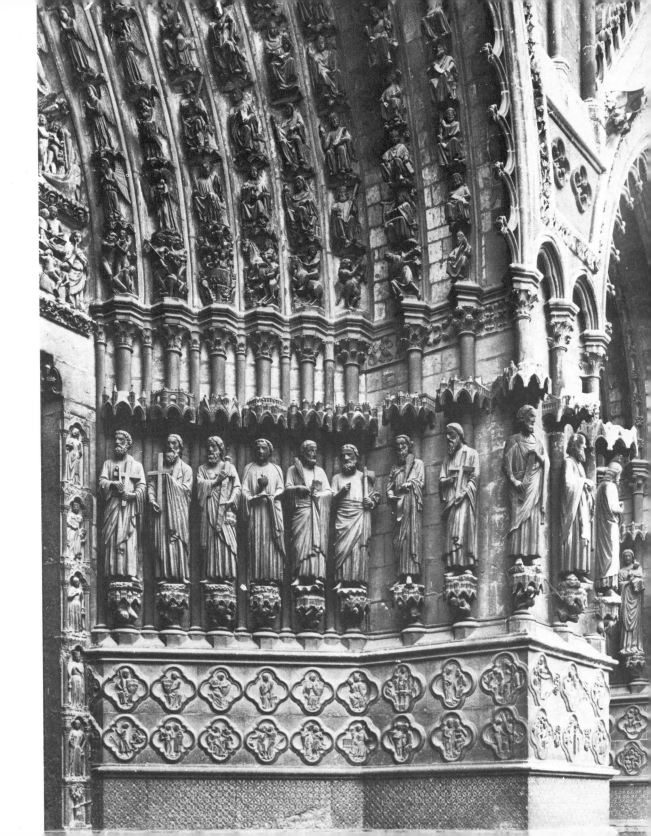

Around the middle of the thirteenth century, a significant change took place in the development of church architecture. On the one hand, the new cathedrals were growing so high that the ideas of the architects were outstripping the capacities of the materials and the technical skills available, with the result that, often, vaults which were insufficiently supported collapsed disastrously. On the other hand, in a new period marked by political and social unrest and regroupings, the older, slow building methods were no longer practical. Thus, the cathedral at Beauvais was begun in 1247 on a gigantic scale; it collapsed, was rebuilt, and finally only the choir was completed. Yet, at the same time, the architectural ideal of the age was changing to the chapel, the direct antithesis of the immense cathedral. True, chapels were made ever larger, but in such cases it was still only as if a cathedral had been reduced to just the choir. The finest example of this is the Sainte-Chapelle in Paris, an imposing, large room built above a hall-like lower church. Its impressive effect comes from its slender architectural members, which form a delicate framework for the luminous stained-glass windows, which are among the oldest surviving in Paris. Below the windows, the wall is divided into an elegant arcade whose gilding and inlays of opaque glass and enamel make it gleam like a precious reliquary.

The Massacre of the Innocents, detail of the tympanum over the portal of the north transept, cathedral of Notre-Dame, Paris. Middle of thirteenth century

Interior of the upper church, Sainte-Chapelle, Paris. ▶ Possibly built by Pierre de Montreuil as the court chapel for the royal palace and consecrated in 1248

Resurrection of the Dead on Judgment Day, detail of the tympanum over the middle door, west portal, cathedral of Saint-Étienne, Bourges. c. 1270–80

Console with personification of Lust and her attribute, a he-goat. Latter half of thirteenth century. Auxerre Cathedral ▶

The representation of the Last Judgment in the tympanum above the central door of the west portal of a cathedral stems from a long tradition with a twofold root, secular and ecclesiastical. For one thing, to enter a church through such a portal already means that the individual has chosen between good and evil. But, also, the west end of a church, either in a projecting porch or directly in front of the portals, was the place where civil transgressions were judged, and the image of the God of Judgment lent a symbolic legitimacy to civil justice. However, for the Scholastic thought of the Gothic age it no longer sufficed to portray the almighty God surrounded, on Judgment Day, by the righteous and by the symbolic animals of the Logos. Such a message, addressed to the men of the time, must of necessity show men themselves in recognizable guise. But since all men would stand naked before God, deprived of all the advantages of their social state on earth, they were depicted nude. After judgment, the righteous were clothed again, because nudity symbolized sin, especially unchastity—a grievously sweet vexation to man, as is shown by the console below with its seductive figure of Lust.

In southern France, Gothic architecture followed an independent tradition in which Catalan traits predominated. From the outside, the cathedral of Albi looks like a massive, invulnerable fortress. Because the abutment piers for the immense vault which covers the single nave are incorporated into the wall itself, and make a series of chapel niches the length of the nave, the exterior surfaces are, for the most part, smooth or rounded. The places where pilasters appear in the interior are marked outside only by semicircular projections which resemble watchtowers. This type of citadel-church is frequent in southern France and Catalonia, where it played a part in the city defenses, a place to retreat to until reinforcements could arrive. Often such churches were built over a stream, so that water would not be lacking in the event of siege.

The Jacobin church in Toulouse is likewise built in brick. Its exterior is unornamented and bare. Reinforced side walls substitute for flying buttresses, since the vault of a hall church does not require an extensive redistribution of stresses. The interior is a rare example of a church with two naves, a plan devised to permit *patres* and *fratres* to worship in equal but separate areas. The unadorned walls of the interior are compensated by the unusually beautiful proportions of the large hall and the vault.

Cathedral of Sainte-Cécile, Albi. This is a hall church without transept, built in red brick. The east choir was begun in 1282 by the Dominican bishop and Grand Inquisitor Bernard de Castanet. The main structure was completed in 1365, but work went on at least until 1480

Interior looking east, church of the Jacobins, ▶ Toulouse. Begun c. 1230, it was completed in 1292 and consecrated in 1385, when the mortal remains of Saint Thomas Aquinas were transported to it

Under pressure from the Capetians, in 1305 the Archbishop of Bordeaux was made Pope Clement V. Because of the unsettled political situation, he and his successors were forced to reside in Avignon, in a "Babylonian captivity of the Church" which lasted until 1377. Clement V made the Dominican monastery his headquarters in Avignon, but his successors built an immense palace in the form of a citadel. The splendid and quite secular character of the papal court made Avignon a great cultural center in southern France in the fourteenth century. The palace was decorated by Simone Martini, Matteo Giovanetti, and others, who constituted a kind of court school of painting; and they introduced the influence of the Italian Early Renaissance which was already in germination and which, from Avignon, spread to the royal courts of Europe.

◄ One of the few surviving frescoes on the theme of the hunt in the study of Pope Clement VI (1342–52) in the wardrobe tower of the Papal Palace at Avignon, built in 1343. Its delight in nature marks it as a transition to the Late Gothic and also announces the beginning of the Italian Renaissance

West façade of the so-called Palais Vieux, Palace of the Popes, Avignon. Built under Benedict XII (1334–42). Note the severe articulation of the wall by pointed arches

View of the town and citadel of Carcassonne. Built between the twelfth and fifteenth centuries over the remains of an earlier citadel. Heavily restored by Violet-le-Duc in the nineteenth century

Portal of the Fort Saint-André, Villeneuve-lès-Avignon, ▶ across the river from Avignon. Built 1362–68 around an already existing Benedictine abbey and a village

The medieval fortresses which today strike us as so picturesque were the scenes of tumultuous conflicts. They were always built at key points of a region in order to survey and defend the important approaches and the commercial roads. The hill on which Carcassonne was built had already been the site of a Gallo-Roman citadel which was later occupied by the Visigoths and expanded. Stretches of wall from both those periods were incorporated into the late-medieval fortress. In the Albigensian Crusades, Simon de Montfort laid unsuccessful siege to the town, which later came under the French crown and was further fortified under Louis IX and Philip the Bold. The city was protected by a massive double ring of walls whose inner ring is much higher than the outer. An enemy who succeeded in getting across the first wall would be trapped helplessly in the broad moat between the two rings, and the curve of the walls and the overhanging round towers made it possible to shoot at an invader from the side and even, at certain places, from the back. Inside the city walls was the strongly fortified castle of the Count which, in extreme necessity, could serve as a final place of retreat. The only access to the city is by a narrow highroad which leads through a huge fortified barbican gate, above which is set a statue of the Madonna, patroness and protectress of the city.

West front, Lincoln Cathedral. The central part of the façade and the lower parts of the towers are Romanesque-Norman, the broad upper structure is Early Gothic of c. 1250

Nave, cathedral of Saint Peter, Exeter. The Gothic building, begun c. 1280, incorporates the walls of the Romanesque-Norman church of the beginning of the twelfth century ▶

Through its Norman architecture of the twelfth century, England made an essential contribution to the development of the French Gothic cathedral: already around 1104–30, cross-rib vaulting had been used in Durham Cathedral. In the thirteenth century the influence flowed the other way, and England took from France the inspiration for its own unique formal vocabulary. Even the ground plans of English cathedrals have their own peculiarities. In contrast to the French Gothic tendency to unify all the separate spatial components, in England the structure is composed of separate, diversified units. Further, English churches often have more than one transept as well as chapels let into the walls, and there is an imposing tower at the crossing whose substructure is in essential harmony with the impression of space given by the nave. In that respect, the Norman tradition lived on. Most striking is the marked emphasis on articulation through decoration. On the exterior, this is seen especially in the breadth of the façade which often, as at Lincoln, is much wider than the nave and aisles which lie behind it. In the interior, there is a stress on deeply projecting fan vaulting, as at Exeter whose typical "Decorated Style" unifies the entire interior.

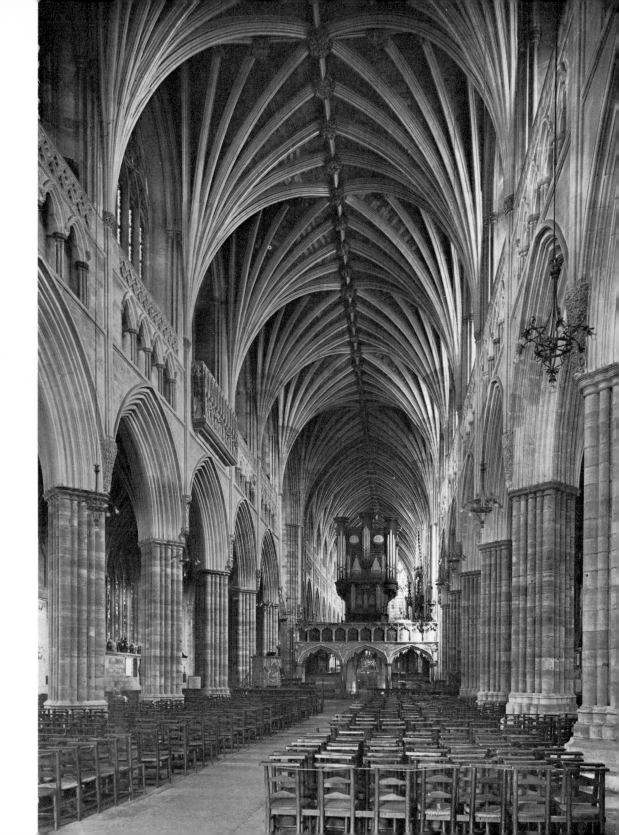

West front (above) and view of the crossing (facing page), cathedral of Saint Andrew, Wells. Begun by Bishop Reginald de Bohun c. 1186, completed by 1239, and the upper parts of the towers added in the fourteenth and fifteenth centuries

Wells Cathedral is one of the great achievements of English Gothic. In the broad, screenlike organization of the west front, with towers to either side of the church rather than constituting part of it as in France, there is one of the forms of horizontal arrangement to which English art, in general, tends. Statues are not confined to the portals but appear all over the façade, and the portals themselves are merely inconspicuous openings in the base of the building. In the interior, it was found necessary after 1338 to reinforce the piers bearing the weight of the tower over the crossing. The result was a fantastically ingenious solution which created an entirely new focal point for the eye: strainer arches were placed on three sides under the lantern, propping up the piers from top to bottom. The main arch is crowned by a Late Gothic crucifix such as, in most English and continental cathedrals, hung instead above the altar just before the crossing. Typical also is the continuous horizontal articulation of the nave.

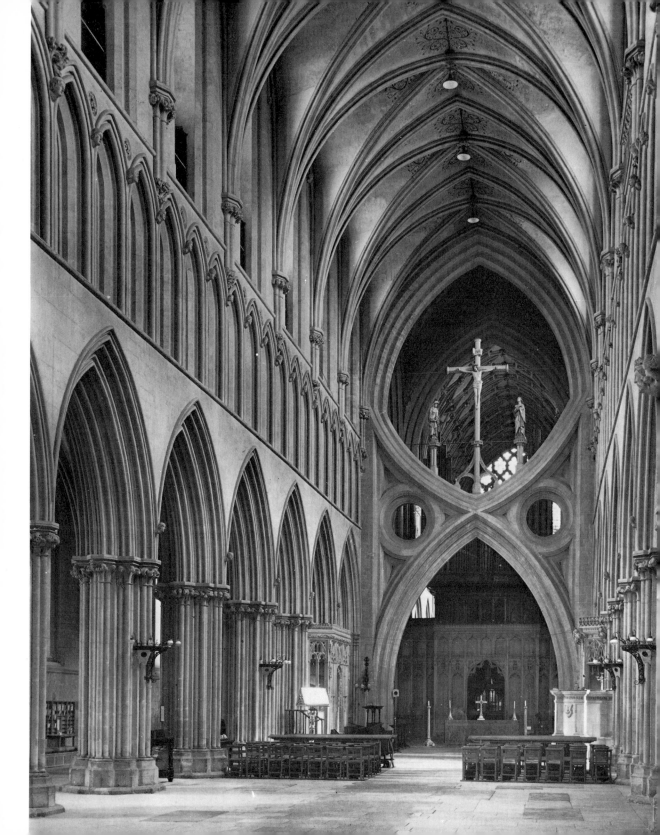

Here are two examples of the tendency, typical of England in the Late Middle Ages, to conceive church interiors in terms of highly imaginative decoration. When the Norman crossing tower at Ely collapsed in 1322, the old foundations of the tower were dismantled and an octagonal vault was built to span the entire width of the nave and aisles. The construction itself is less daring than it looks, because the vault was built of wood. From the zenith of the lantern, a Christ set in the center of a star gazes down on the nave. The impressiveness is enhanced by the contrast between the bright light of the lantern vault with its many windows as opposed to the fanlike ribs, lying in shadow, which run from the piers of the nave to support the cupola of the lantern. This is one of the last works in the so-called Decorated Style whose basic aim, as the name implies, was elaborate decoration. In contrast, the Chapel of Henry VII in Westminster Abbey is typical of the final phase of medieval English Gothic. Its decoration is nonfunctional, without relation to the interior space, and everything conspires to emphasize the Gothic principle of verticality, with the decorative elements of the vault hanging down like stalactites. There is, in fact, an impression of crystalline hardness in this chapel, a masterpiece of what is called the Perpendicular Style.

Tomb of Edward the Black Prince. 1377–80. Gilt latten. Canterbury Cathedral

◀ Tomb of a Knight Templar (destroyed in the war). c. 1250. Marble. Temple Church, London

Like English architecture, English sculpture also shows a strong tendency to severity in over-all design, which is combined with a highly varied treatment of all details. The sculpture on church façades was, in part, very much influenced by France, though it could not match the quality of its models. However, it is among tomb statues that one finds genuine masterworks. The high points of the Gothic age are the royal tombs in Westminster Abbey and, even more, these two austere effigies of English knights.

NOTTINGHAM WORKSHOPS. *The Holy Trinity*, also known as the *Throne of Mercy*. Beginning of fourteenth century. Alabaster relief. Sankt Maria zur Wiese, Soest (Westphalia)

◀ South wing of the Great Cloister, cathedral of the Holy Trinity, Gloucester. The east wing, built in 1351–57, has the earliest fully developed example of fan-tracery vaulting

In the latter part of the thirteenth century, alabaster became a favorite material of English sculptors, and even life-sized recumbent effigies on tombs were made from that stone. Nottingham was the center for alabaster sculptors, and its alabaster wall-reliefs and carved altars with small alabaster figures were exported all over the Christian world, especially to northern Germany, western France, and Spain. One of the finest such works is the so-called Throne of Mercy in Soest, an iconographical innovation of the twelfth century, in which the Trinity is combined with the Passion of Christ: God the Father, enthroned, broods over the Cross on which hangs the body of the Son, while above Christ's head soars the dove of the Holy Ghost.

◄ Polygonal choir with ambulatory and radiating apsidal chapels, Magdeburg Cathedral. Begun 1209, upper story built after 1220

Nave, cathedral of Sankt Paul, Münster (Westphalia). 1225–63. Note the broadly spacious hall-church character within a basilica plan

French Gothic influence made its way into Germany very slowly, resisted by the native tradition in architecture. One of the major Gothic cathedrals was built in Magdeburg to replace the cathedral of Otto the Great which had burned down in 1207. In its ground plan and elevation, it is clearly influenced by the Burgundian churches with their apsidal chapels radiating off the choir. But in the heaviness and powerful massiveness of its articulation one sees that the late Hohenstaufen tradition was still strong. Characteristic are the simple openings of the windows and the emphasis on strong, solid wall supports which stand out markedly from the outer walls. The traditional values survived in the Münster cathedral also: the compressed proportions despite the spaciousness, the vigorous effect of the wall masses, the heavy and typically Westphalian domical vault.

This is one of the earliest panel paintings in Germany. Designed as an altarpiece, it marks the beginning of a rich development out of the existing style of wall painting. A triple arcade, like those one finds encircling the base of a choir, serves as a frame for a picture whose soaring figures seem almost like a fresco seen behind an altar. In style there are certain affinities with the wall paintings in Sankt Nikolai in Soest and in Sankt Kunibert, Cologne. But the finely worked frame, gilded arcades, and gold background into which the names of the saints are embossed, all recall also the reliquaries of the preceding period, and it is certain that such reliquaries were of considerable influence on the origins of panel painting.

In accord with the medieval conception of the church as a replica on earth of Heaven, and like the Ottonian altar frontal from Basel (now in the Cluny Museum, Paris), these arcades are meant to define the scene as Heaven. Gold backgrounds had been used ever since the Byzantine cupolas, and even earlier, to emphasize the otherworldly character, which here is indicated also by the angels painted above the columns. Beneath the central arch is the Trinity in the form of a Throne of Mercy, while Mary and John appear in the lateral arcades in a way familiar from Last Judgments, imploring the God of Judgment for mercy for mankind. In contrast to the meditative mysticism of the Throne of Mercy in Soest (page 51), here the representation is meant to be apocalyptic, a direct image of the final destiny of humanity, and is related to the consummation of the Eucharist effected on the altar beneath it. The vehement treatment of the drapery, with its angular folds in the so-called "jagged style" which was typical of painting in the middle of the century, is in contrast with the monumental rigor of the picture as a whole. Although the architectural framework is still Romanesque in form, the body of Christ hanging on the cross is already Gothic in its portrayal of a body from which all life has fled; and Christ is no longer the kingly victor over death as in Romanesque art. Yet the dead Christ here is only one part of a total image which is a powerful, graphic representation of the divine hierarchy.

Triptych by an unknown artist of Westphalia or Cologne, formerly in the church of Sankt Maria zur Wiese, Soest. Before 1250. Tempera on oak panel, 28 × 47¹/₄″. State Museums, Berlin-Dahlem

Left: *The Blessed*, detail of the tympanum on the facing page.
Below: *Head of a Damned King*, detail of the same tympanum

In Bamberg, a new cathedral was begun after 1185 on the ground plan of an older cathedral, and it was completed and consecrated in 1237. The Romanesque tradition was still followed in the square schematism of the nave and in the form of the east choir. However, the new spirit of the French Gothic is plain to read in the Cistercian west choir and the west towers, the latter influenced by the cathedral of Laon—and this is true of most of the sculpture. The statues, which were carved by a sculptor who must certainly have learned his art in France, are set into traditional Romanesque arched embrasures. What is characteristic of this sculptor is the way he compresses a scene into a very narrow space which does not actually delimit it but, instead, seems to burst outward with the tension. He contrived, too, highly convincing gestures and facial expressions and, above all, had a feeling for the power of self-contained volumes much like that which one finds in architecture of the time.

The Last Judgment, tympanum of the main portal *(Fürstenportal)*, Bamberg Cathedral. c. 1235–37

To the left of the Christ of Judgment on the tympanum (above) are the Blessed with the Instruments of the Passion—the Cross, Lance, and Crown of Thorns. At the far left are the human souls taken up into Heaven. At the right, the damned souls struggle in the chains of Satan. Beneath the feet of Christ, hopeful souls arise from their graves, and Mary and John kneel at either side as their intercessors.

Prophets, on the choir screen of the east choir (the Saint George choir), Bamberg Cathedral. c. 1230. Facing page: detail of the head of Jonah from the middle group

On the exterior of the stone balustrades around the choir in Bamberg there is a unique and unprecedented iconographical program: twelve prophets on the north side, twelve Apostles on the south side are presented, two by two, in arched embrasures. There are twenty-four figures in all, the canonical number of the Elders who surround the throne of the Apocalypse. Each pair is engaged in an energetic dialogue which mounts to heights of spiritual tension, with expressions and gestures of an extraordinary vehemence. The drama is conveyed by means of extreme poses: in the central group of Jonah and Hosea, it is as if one figure had pursued the other who suddenly turned back to resume the argument. This is mirrored also in the tortuous coils of the draperies and in the dialectical interweaving of gestures and folds of drapery between one figure and its companion. The artists may have borrowed such traits from something like the north portal at Chartres (page 19), but here they intensified the formal aspect by stressing the dramatic content.

King on Horseback, on the pier to the left of the choir, Bamberg Cathedral. c. 1233–35

World-famous as is this royal horseman, much about him is still a mystery. It scarcely seems likely that the original intention was to place the statue on the pier to the left of the choir. That position makes it seem as if the king had ridden by and suddenly reined in his horse before the sanctuary, and is probably the result of some change in the original plan. Yet, the place where the statue now stands is made to seem exactly right precisely because of the horse's movement: the forelegs are already at rest, while the rear legs are still taking the last step. Add to this the fact that the horseman himself is weaponless, as a warrant of his peaceable intentions. His presence in the church suggests that he may represent some saintly monarch, perhaps Constantine the Great, in whose tradition and succession the medieval German emperors claimed to act. The contemporary clothing and manner, and the way the Hohenstaufen ideal of the sovereign is embodied in the figure, also suggest that some contemporary ruler may have wished to use this effigy to legitimize his claim to be the heir of Constantine. This may well be, because in the Middle Ages the classical equestrian statue of Marcus Aurelius (which formerly stood in front of the Lateran Palace, but was removed to its present post on the Capitol in 1538) was believed to portray Constantine and, as such, had been copied repeatedly ever since the time of Theoderic.

NAUMBURG MASTER. *The Last Supper*, on the rood loft, Naumburg Cathedral. After 1250

The unknown artist who has been called the Naumburg Master, after the place where he worked, ranks among the greatest of German sculptors. Trained in France, traces of his work have been made out in the choir screen at Chartres, in Noyon, Amiens, and perhaps even in Metz, from where he can be followed through Mainz to Naumburg. There, for the rood loft of the cathedral, he sculpted a seven-part epic poem in stone, of which five scenes have survived. Each scene is set in a well-defined spatial unity, as if on a stage. The sacred events are treated in a highly individual manner. In the Last Supper, for instance, there are only six figures instead of the traditional thirteen. The monumental repose of the Christ in the center makes Him stand out in isolation among the agitated Apostles, whose eating and drinking allude to the bread and wine of the Eucharist. The action focuses on the figure at the extreme right, and the larger meaning of the event is expressed through him. His bald head is covered by a prayer shawl, and his gaze is intent with a presentiment of the awesome event to come. His right hand grasps tensely the fish in the bowl (the early Christian symbol for Christ) while his left hand tugs at the tablecloth as if to draw it away from the betrayer at the opposite end of the table, to whom the folds of the cloth, as well as the hand of Christ, draw one's eye.

NAUMBURG MASTER. *The Patrons of the Cathedral*, west choir, Naumburg Cathedral. Facing page: *Ekkehard and Uta*. Right: *Wilhelm of Komburg*. 1250–60

A documentary source of 1249 explains why, in the west choir of Naumburg Cathedral, there are eleven statues of patrons of the church, though all of those personages had lived two centuries before their portraits were made and none of them were saints (one was even a murderer). It appears that they were intended as an example to contemporary patrons of the church and also as a memorial to the family of the prince-bishop who founded the cathedral.

The statues are not lined up in a row, like statues on portals, but are either grouped in pairs or singly. What unites them all is the area between them and the altar where the Eucharist is celebrated, because all of them, in their humanity, participate in the sacrificial Mass unto all eternity. In that respect, they symbolize the medieval conception of the sanctity of good works, which in the thought of the time gave man the right to hope for Paradise, that Paradise of which the church itself is a symbol. Thus, two notions are tightly linked, one of political sovereignty, the other of religious devotion. With his masterly feeling for dramatic effect, the Naumburg Master created here something almost theatrical. He could not have known what these personages really looked like, nor was that even a matter of interest in his time, but he synthesized individual and universal traits into something as expressive as a portrait. By bringing together diverse characteristics, he revealed certain latent personal conflicts and tensions, and thereby endowed his personages with what seems to be a capacity for choice which is suggestive of some personal drama; for centuries now, men have puzzled over just what that drama may have been. Each figure has its individual bearing, its own characteristic gesture which sums up its inner essence. This is true, above all, of the faces with their quite personal expressions of oppression, tension, determination, resignation, or naïve trust. Seldom has human character been caught with such breadth and set down forever in the form of art.

View of Freiburg, anonymous painting on glass from the middle of the nineteenth century. Neues Schloss, Baden-Baden

Ambulatory and apsidal chapels, minster of Unsere ▶
Liebe Frau, Freiburg im Breisgau

As early as the twelfth century, the Upper Rhine region between Basel and Strasbourg had become one of the richest artistic centers of the Middle Ages, and it remained so right up to the beginning of the sixteenth century. There, in churches built out of the characteristic red sandstone of the Rhine Valley, each phase of the Middle Ages has left its mark. The minster at Freiburg, unlike most cathedrals of the time, was not built as an episcopal seat but, instead, as a communal parish church. The great west tower rose as an emblem of the city high above the houses clustered around it, houses which have since been victims of war. A painting on glass done in the Romantic period shows us what the city looked like a century ago, when it was still virtually as it had been ever since the end of the Middle Ages.

Madonna on the *trumeau* of the main entrance of the porch under the west tower, Freiburg Minster. Beneath her feet is the sleeping Jesse, the ancestor of Christ, and from his body grows a tree whose tendrils surround the Madonna and whose topmost branches frame the scenes from the Passion and the Last Judgment in the great arch over the portal. c. 1280–90

The minster at Freiburg was one of the first nonprovincial religious monuments erected entirely as a parish church by the citizenry itself. Nothing recalls the original Romanesque structure except the transept and the two towers rising above it. The Gothic parts are entirely distinct new units added to the old ones. The heavy, squat forms of the nave show the influence of a Burgundian school of architecture, the variant of the French Gothic which was most akin to the German feeling for form. Around 1280 the great west tower was begun, and the basic idea behind it was not ecclesiastical but civic: it was conceived as a monument of the city itself. Although many later periods had a hand in its construction, the tower is a thoroughly unified structure of great beauty. One of the earlier architects built the heavy substructure and entrance porch, which were completed around 1300. The star-shaped gallery over the square crossing of the lower structure was joined perfectly, by a later master, to the octagon of the tower which soars above the rooftops. If this tower has been called one of the most beautiful towers in Christendom, no small credit goes to the openwork stone spire. The tower changed the whole appearance of the city, and remains its chief landmark. In 1354 the cornerstone was laid for a new, higher Gothic choir, in the construction of which a member of the Parler family was involved, but the choir was not consecrated until 1513. Seen from the outside, its height creates a happy and harmonious balance with the tall tower (see page 64).

While the plain nave was conceived in terms of the Christian community, as an expression of the Church itself, the tower and choir have an additional meaning which relates to the civil community. The deep porch is not only an entrance but also a symbol of the Last Judgment, and its wall decoration bears this out. Along with the allusion to the genealogy of Christ on the portal, there are the Vices and Virtues, allegorical personifications of worldly temptations and Christian teachings which offer graphic images of the alternatives between which man must choose. The very fine altarpieces in the choir chapels of the ambulatory were contributed by wealthy burghers, and the craft guilds donated the stained-glass windows which bear the insignia of their craft. Thus, the interior of the minster represents the collaboration between different styles and periods, the various arts, and also the separate social classes. In that respect, it is a true symbol of late-medieval Christianity, an all-dominant force which brought together, in unity, every aspect of both religious and social life.

Lust is presented here as a symbol of wordly temptation, the embodiment of lasciviousness vainly trying to conceal her shame beneath a goat's hide. Next to her stands an angel, whose smile reassures the sinners that they may yet be saved. Beneath baldachins, the figures stand on an architectural structure composed of Gothic arches, and this runs all around the walls of the porch. Below it there are benches for the participants in the assemblies which take place here, and the gaze of most of the statues is directed downward, as if to focus on the congregation below.

Among the most significant works of medieval architectonic sculpture are those on the cathedral of Strasbourg. Done at various times throughout the thirteenth century, they testify to a strong, continuous local tradition. At Strasbourg it was the south portal which was devoted to the Last Judgment. There, the wise judge Solomon on the central pillar is flanked by the representatives of the old and the new faiths, the Church in triumph and the Synagogue in defeat. These statues mark the birth of German Gothic monumental sculpture. When the motif of the old covenant overcome by Christianity was used in France, where it first appeared, it was usually given an abstract presentation. In Germany, however, it was transformed into an action in which human sympathies are engaged: in defeat humanity is greater than in proud triumph.

The Prince of the World and a Foolish Virgin, on the right portal of the west front, Strasbourg Cathedral. c. 1280

The wall statues at Strasbourg followed a new program for façades which was quite unlike those used in the classical French Gothic cathedrals. Old Testament prophets flank the main entrance. On the left portal, virtuous heroines overcome the Vices in somewhat theatrical manner, while on the right portal appears the parable of the Wise and the Foolish Virgins. Such motifs played a great role in the moralistic literature of the time, and they were used in churches as symbols of the two basic choices set before the Christian as he entered the House of God.

Head of the *Synagogue*, south portal, Strasbourg Cathedral. After 1230. Museum of the Cathedral, Strasbourg (the statue now on the façade is a copy)

Town Hall, Stralsund. Fourteenth century. In the background is seen the tower of the
church of Sankt Nikolai

West front, Cistercian church,
Chorin. 1273–1300. This is the
most important example of the
brick architecture of North Germany

As in southern France, a distinct style of architecture using brick developed in Holstein, Brandenburg, the
northern Netherlands, Denmark, and, later, in Bavaria, and was inspired primarily by Lombard models.
The previously prepared bricks made possible a special style of construction characterized by markedly flat
surfaces, broad articulation, and avoidance of complicated sculptural ornamentation. The bricks themselves
provided whatever decoration there was. Arches for windows and portals were assembled from stones rounded
off in advance. The flat surfaces obtained by this method corresponded to a tendency to construct broad
façades, and this led to a highly imaginative treatment in the North German brick buildings especially. Often
the façade was conceived quite independently of the building itself, as in the Stralsund town hall where the
six-gabled façade rises high above the three-gabled building lying behind it.

West front, Orvieto Cathedral. Original design by Lorenzo Maitani 1310–30, continued in 1347 by Andrea Pisano and in 1354 by Andrea Orcagna, who did the rose window, and completed only at the beginning of the seventeenth century; mosaics done by various artists from the fourteenth to the nineteenth century (the earlier ones now heavily restored)

Nave, looking toward the choir, Santa Maria Novella, Florence. The church was built 1246–1360, the nave begun in 1279

The term "Latinized Gothic" has been applied to those Italian buildings of the Late Middle Ages in which the local architectural tradition came to terms with the conceptions of the French Gothic. However, Italy never took up the design of the typical French façade with its twin towers, because ever since the Early Middle Ages the bell tower or campanile had been a separate building in Italy. Nor were Italian façades conceived in spatial terms but rather, for the most part, as co-ordinated surfaces in which the only divisions were smaller fields which usually were filled in with mosaics or shallow-relief plaques. This can be seen at Orvieto, where the reliefs on the four piers of the portal present the most fully developed sculptural program of any Italian Gothic façade. Interiors likewise were treated differently. The native feeling for structure was indifferent to Northern architecture with its bundle pillars which soar up ecstatically. Instead, spacious sunlit halls were articulated by widely spaced pillars, and the inner space was delimited expressively by unadorned walls which made no attempt at transparency.

These churches in Pisa and Assisi are among the gems of Gothic architecture in Italy. They have in common a clear emphasis on basic structure. In Pisa the fundamental geometrical design is not affected by the decorative elements added as trimming. At Assisi, the open, unobstructed rectangular hall has uninterrupted flat walls designed to hold frescoes by Cimabue and the Giotto school which are among the masterpieces of the Western world. The acceptance of some aspects of the French Gothic formal vocabulary had no effect on the Italian feeling for physical space. That was something inherited from Roman Antiquity, and its basic tendencies led without interruption into the Early Renaissance. In Assisi, especially, the elements related to those of the French Gothic—the cross-ribbed vault, the gallery above the lower zone, the transept intersecting the nave—are almost seamlessly incorporated into the clear, open basic structure.

Santa Maria della Spina, Pisa. 1230–1323. The exterior walls are covered with marble in two colors

Upper church, San Francesco, Assisi. 1228–53. Frescoed by Giotto and assistants c. 1290–1300

NICOLA PISANO (c. 1225–c. 1287). *Nativity*. 1266–68.
Marble relief on the pulpit, Siena Cathedral

GIOVANNI PISANO (c. 1248–after 1314). Marble pulpit.
1302–10. Pisa Cathedral

In the thirteenth century, much more emphasis was placed on preaching, and the sermon came to be delivered from a pulpit in proximity to the congregation rather than from the ambo in the sanctuary itself. The great influence in Italy came from the Franciscans and Dominicans, and there the first pulpits were erected in the thirteenth century, whereas in the North they did not come into use for another two centuries. The pulpits were decorated with statues and reliefs which combined to make up a Scholastic moralizing program of the sort found in France on church portals. Italian sculpture of the time, in particular that of Nicola Pisano, consciously imitated Antique models, a classicizing trend fostered by Emperor Frederick II in Apulia, the province from which Nicola seems to have come. Freestanding figures reveal their debt to classical Roman statues, and the reliefs on pulpits show that there was a deliberate return to the relief style of ancient sarcophaguses in which the numerous figures were presented pictorially, moving energetically in space.

GIOVANNI PISANO. *Allegory of Chastity*, on the marble pulpit in Pisa Cathedral. Here the sculptor imitated the Hellenistic statue known as the *Venus Medicea*

Equestrian statue of Cangrande della Scala (d. 1330), from his tomb. Museo di Castelvecchio, Verona

The tombs of the Scaligers, lords over the marches of Verona and Treviso from 1304 to 1387, are among the most impressive funerary monuments of medieval Italy. Beneath high baldachins set up on columns lie the sarcophaguses of the warlords who, themselves, appear on the roofs of the tombs, fully armed and on horseback, some attended by angels and personifications of the dead ruler's virtues, others by warrior-saints who keep watch over the dead.

ANDREA DI CIONE, called OR-
CAGNA. *Annunciation*, detail
from the base of the tabernacle
opposite. Marble relief against
blue vitreous inlay

ANDREA DI CIONE, called ORCAGNA (c. 1308–68). Tabernacle in the church ▶
of Orsanmichele, Florence. c. 1349–59. The painting of the *Madonna Enthroned
with Angels* is by BERNARDO DADDI (d. c. 1348), 1346–47

Orsanmichele was originally a grain market, open on all sides. In 1380 walls were constructed and the building
made into a church. Thus, initially, Orcagna's tabernacle and baldachin stood in an open hall as an independent architectural structure. As we see it today, there is a kind of curious reversal: one goes through a strongly
articulated, hall-like interior with its heavy pillars and round wall-arches to stand before one of the loveliest
pieces of architecture of the Italian Gothic, one which seems to be intended for the exterior of a church and
is half tabernacle, half triumphal arch. It frames a painting of the Madonna, and her life is recounted in reliefs
all round the base of the tabernacle. Glowing colored inlays fill in spaces in the architectural framework
which, in the French Gothic, were left open, and the colored inlays behind the reliefs create a convincing
sense of depth.

Milan Cathedral is the largest and most contradictory edifice of the Italian Gothic, of which it is nevertheless a high point. Its ground plan is like that of the double-aisled cathedral in Cologne, which likewise was not completed until modern times. For building material, marble was imported from Candoglia on Lake Maggiore, but the Lombard builders were familiar only with the bricks used locally, and over and over again their inexperience led to difficulties. As a result, outstanding German and French master masons had to be called in, among them Heinrich Parler III, Ulrich von Ensingen, and Jean Mignot, to solve the problems connected with the vaulting. Their ideas met with resistance from the local builders, and one after the other they withdrew from the project, which then went along as best it could until new insuperable difficulties again made it necessary to call in experienced foreigners. So it is so much the more miraculous that the exterior of the cathedral ever did achieve the harmonious unity we see today, in the choir in particular with its wonderfully articulated tracery windows, its transparent balustrades rising to the tower over the crossing, and its filigree-like openwork buttresses. One of the later sculptors made the ultimate ironic comment on the building's history: on one of the pillars of the façade he carved a relief of the Tower of Babel.

Santa Maria Nascente, the cathedral of Milan. Begun before 1386. Choir, transept, and a few bays of the nave completed by 1452. Building finally completed at end of nineteenth century

Ducal Palace, Mantua.
Begun 1302

To understand the diverse forms which the basic structure of a Northern Italian palace could take, one must compare the Ducal Palace of Mantua (preceding page) with the Doge's Palace in Venice. In the latter, the upper structure seems to mirror Venice itself in its inversion of all the customary static relationships: a heavy, closed block of building rests on a delicate, filigree-like, openwork support. However, the proportions we see today are somewhat falsified. The level of the piazza has been raised, thereby covering over the lower two feet of the ground-floor arcade, so that now the entire solid block appears to be top-heavy. Matteo Raverti, to whom some of the architectonic decoration is due, used similar forms in the Ca' d'Oro, one of the most splendid of the Venetian palaces. The decoration in gleaming white Istrian limestone was once in part gilded, whence the name of "the golden palace." In Venice, with its world-wide commercial activities, an important role was played by influences from Islamic architecture; Europe could offer little help in solving the problems of the relation between architecture and water, except for an occasional citadel built on an island. Here, the total effect of the structure is completed visually by the ceaselessly moving reflections in the flowing waters of the canals.

Palace of the Doges, Venice. 1340 on

Ca' d'Oro, on the Grand Canal, Venice. ▶
Completed 1434

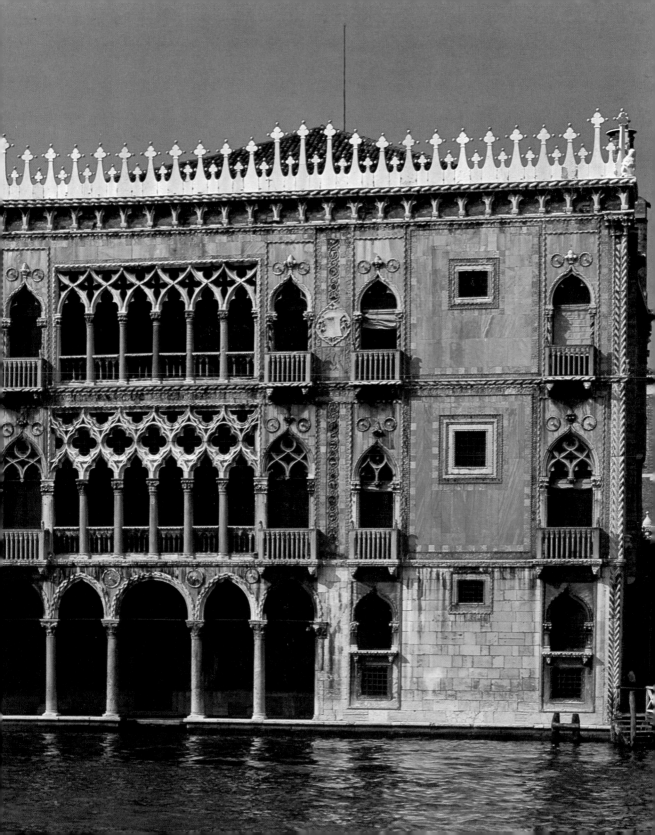

GIOTTO (c. 1266/67–1337). *Madonna Enthroned with Angels*, from the church of Ognissanti, Florence. c. 1310. Tempera and gilding on panel, 10′ 8³/₄″ × 6′ 7⁷/₈″. Uffizi Gallery, Florence

▼

The work of Simone Martini, an important younger contemporary of Giotto, is more Gothic, and represents a return to the almost disembodied character of Gothic art. Nevertheless it carries on the fundamental lessons of Giotto. The poses and gestures are expressions of human feelings, and between Lippo Memmi's saints, who stand like statues at either side, the mystery of the sacred event is brought out as a clear, precisely characterized occurrence.

SIMONE MARTINI (1284–1344) and LIPPO MEMMI (active 1317–47). *The Annunciation.* 1333. Tempera and gilding on panel, c. 9′ 10″ × 11′ 5³/₄″. Uffizi Gallery, Florence. Dated and signed by both artists, the figures to either side are generally attributed to Lippo Memmi. In the gold background are embossed the words *Ave gratia plena, Dominus tecum* (Hail, Mary, full of grace; the Lord is with thee). The carved and gilded frame in Gothic architectural forms is superimposed on the painting and becomes part of it

With Giotto there came into Western art a new conception of the nature of a picture. The impressive character of his *Madonna Enthroned* both fulfills and transcends the criteria of the Byzantine tradition. The ivory tower, which in the Lorettine Litany is a symbol of Mary, rises above her throne in the form of a French Gothic baldachin which is itself a symbol of Heaven, as is also the gold background of the painting. The Madonna is surrounded by angels and, behind them, are four prophets of the Old Testament. The image is presented in an empirical perspective which centers on the Madonna, though the focal lines are not based on mathematically determined laws. All the accessory figures likewise lead the eye to the Madonna but are smaller in size, overtowered by the massive contours of her head and shoulders and by the haloed head of the Christ child. The organization of a picture according to a central focal point and the elimination of all unimportant details were both innovations. So too were the emphasis on volumes, the impression of a heavy and lifelike body, the modeling of the heads, the textural realism of the draperies, and the secure equilibrium between flat planes and effects of perspective. The sacred figures have been liberated from the supernatural spirituality of earlier art to become images of elevated dignity which, at the same time, have a material solidity and a new feeling for realism. The new notion of beauty in art thereby introduced was that of a spiritual content given visual expression by purely pictorial means, and this in itself represents a major change in the relationships of art.

◀ PAOLO VENEZIANO (c. 1290–before 1362).
Coronation of the Virgin. First half of the
fourteenth century. Tempera and gilding
on panel, $38^5/_8 \times 24^3/_4''$. Academy, Venice

In Venice, painting, like architecture, remained more closely tied to Byzantine tradition than elsewhere in Italy. But there were
typically Venetian traits also: a feeling for
decorative surfaces and a coloristic sensitivity
which enhances the precious luster of the
details. The gold lines of the borders of the
garments follow their own course, independent of any sense of depth, just as the gold
patterns of the draperies remain unaffected
by the modeling of the figure or by any pleats
and folds. Only the base of the throne shows
the new feeling for space which, otherwise,
seems consciously rejected in this painting.
In the fourteenth century, Gothic art turned
its back on the feeling for reality which
Giotto had attained, and Giotto's lesson remained barren until Masaccio, a hundred
years later.

Burgos Cathedral, Spain. Southwest façade begun by French master
masons, the two towers of the façade completed 1442–52 by the
German architect Johannes of Cologne. The persistence of the
Gothic architectural tradition well into the sixteenth century is
shown by the tower over the crossing erected in 1568

In the eleventh century there began the liberation of Spain from its Arab overlords; and although the final
reconquest took many more centuries, there occurred during that time a lively exchange between Islamic
and Christian intellectual achievements. Foreign pilgrims traveled to Santiago de Compostela in such numbers
that the road they took came to be called in Spain the *camino francés*, and influences flowed in both directions.
Arabic science played a great role in the French universities which were founded around 1200. Influence from
the Île-de-France is seen most clearly in the great cathedrals erected on Spanish soil, whereas other types of
buildings reveal much more the influence of Burgundy and southern France, as a result of the monasteries
and churches built by the Cistercians, who won a foothold in Spain in the second half of the twelfth century.

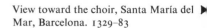

◀ The star vault in the crossing tower,
Burgos Cathedral. Completed 1568

The cathedral of Burgos shows especially clearly how, even after Spain had been won back for Christendom, an Islamic feeling for decoration lived on. The crossing tower has rich sculptural figurative decoration in stucco, and its star vault is composed of a geometrical, linear, filigree-like ribbing. The Gothic spirit remained viable in Burgos for a long time. Through additions and extensions, the original design of the cathedral was almost completely altered, and it became a luxuriant mirror of the most diverse historical styles. On the other hand, the sober, austere aspect of the Gothic is seen in Santa Maria del Mar in Barcelona. There, a broad hall-like interior is opened up spatially by a chain of chapels between the wall piers, with the result that the unity and immensity of the main area are accentuated. Severely unadorned octagonal supports crown the dimly illuminated nave whose walls extend straight up almost to the vaults. The nave has much in common with those of the southern French hall churches in Toulouse and Albi.

Descent from the Cross, from Tahull. Twelfth century. Wood, height of the figures 48–66″. Museo de Arte de Cataluña, Barcelona

In the Catalan sculpture of Spain it is almost impossible to distinguish rigorously between Romanesque and Gothic styles. Traits typical of the twelfth century survived well into the thirteenth. Characteristic are the broadly laid-out compositions and the sense of powerful movement in figures which, however, also have a monumental repose. Although the influence of French cathedral sculpture finally made itself felt in those statues connected with architecture, other sculpture remained more closely tied to the native tradition which continued to be nourished by folk art and, in consequence, is difficult to date on purely stylistic grounds.

The design of secular fortified buildings in the Middle Ages was generally determined more by practical considerations than by architectural criteria, so here too one cannot make any sharp distinction between the styles of the twelfth and the thirteenth centuries. What differences there were came about more through new techniques of warfare than through any architectural concepts. The systems of attack and defense remained essentially the same through centuries, and so stylistic changes must be sought more in architectural details than in the design of the over-all structure.

That is why a citadel like Castel del Monte seems so much the more significant. Its general plan is clearly Gothic, even though, by its nature, a fortress cannot enhance its walls with tall windows and arches. In contrast to the square or circular ground plans of the Romanesque, here—as in many church towers—the new spirit is seen in the octagon form with its prismatic structure which creates a play of light and shadow on the exterior walls. Castel del Monte not only uses an octagonal ground plan but also, at each of its eight corners, has octagonal watchtowers which project out in such a way as to make it possible to trap an invader as if within pincers. Each wall has only a small Gothic window affording a view of the countryside. Although the exterior is stern and forbidding, the octagonal inner court with its Gothic-arched loggias is richly decorated and airy and, as a direct influence from the Cistercian style, the rooms are vaulted with cross-ribbing.

Castel del Monte, the hunting castle of the Hohenstaufen Emperor Frederick II in Apulia. c. 1240

The citadel of Kantara, northwest coast of Cyprus. Begun 1228/29. Set on a rocky cliff falling away abruptly on all sides, some 2,200 feet above sea level, the outer wall follows the irregular line of the rocks and is reinforced by towers and bastions on the south and southeast fronts. At the right can be seen the cistern which is braced by powerful buttresses

The Crusaders carried the influence of the Gothic to the Middle East, and in Syria and Palestine they founded Frankish colonies which survived right up to the sudden end of the Crusader domination in 1291. Their extensive fortified settlements were built in Western fashion, the most important of them being the so-called Krak des Chevaliers in Syria.

After the fall of Acre in 1291, the Franks fled from Palestine by way of the sea and found a new home in Cyprus. Richard the Lion-Hearted had already conquered the island in 1191 when his fleet was driven to shelter there from a storm. For the Christians in the East, the island had become their most important base, and later, in their hour of need, it served them as a place to retreat to. The citadel on Cyprus, whose kingdom survived from 1192 to 1473, was built less as a military necessity than as a proud expression in architecture of the Crusaders' sovereignty: to build fortresses was a privilege of the throne and the knightly orders. Erected on mountain cliffs or rocky peaks, such citadels guaranteed dominion over a vast territory. Nevertheless, here the techniques of building fortifications lagged behind until the fifteenth century, when the threat of Turkish invasion had to be countered and Venetian specialists in military architecture were called in to do a thorough-going overhaul and to strengthen the entire system of defenses.

The Bellapais monastery was probably founded by Amaury de Lusignan, King of Jerusalem from 1198 to 1205, and provided a refuge for the monks who fled from the Holy Land at the end of the twelfth century. At the start of the next century the monastery came under the Premonstratensian rule and was enlarged in the reign of King Hugo (1267–84). In the sixteenth century the monks were driven out by the Turks, and the monastery fell into ruin.

Cloister of the Premonstratensian monastery of Bellapais, northern Cyprus. Late twelfth–thirteenth century

Early Gothic crocket capital with leaf buds, Sankt Elisabeth, Marburg

In the Gothic period, capitals were no longer an essential part of the arcades of the lowest zone of a wall, as earlier, but instead were placed high up, between the pier and the supports bearing the weight of the vaulting. Stylized leaf buds were the first motif used, and as time went on, capitals became ever more naturalistic, with flowers and leaves imitated from those in the local surroundings, so that out of this Paradise Garden grew the ribbings of the vault. In the Late Gothic, when the joining of the weight-bearing and downward-thrusting elements was raised higher and the vaulting grew directly out of the piers, this brief tradition died out.

Pier capital depicting the vintage, Reims Cathedral. This is the earliest use of a naturalistic plant motif in the Gothic
▼

Capital with pecking bird and foliage, upper church, Sainte-Chapelle, Paris

Leaf masks are among the most fantastic enigmas that medieval sculptors have left us. At first they were stylized plant growths which, looked at closely, take on the appearance of human faces, much as in the Mannerist art of the late sixteenth century when Arcimboldo built heads out of vegetation. Later they became heads united with the foliage, and finally there were heads in which only headdresses of leaves recall this extraordinary tradition. The motif can be traced back to Late Antiquity. Passed on by provincial Roman art, it survived into the Romanesque art of France and Germany, whence it was carried over into the Gothic until, finally, the Renaissance returned the whole notion to its classical decorative forms.

Just as Christianity adapted pre-Christian practices to its new spiritual needs, assigning to the old demons a place in churches from which they were meant never to stir, so this motif likewise must have recalled the nature demons and tree spirits of the pagan past.

▲
Leaf mask on the console supporting the King on Horseback, Bamberg Cathedral. c. 1235

Leaf mask on a console, Magdeburg Cathedral. c. 1260

HEINRICH PARLER IV, attributed. The so-called
Parler Bust from Cologne. c. 1390. Stone with
traces of old polychrome, height 18$^1/_8$".
Schnütgen Museum, Cologne

Portrait reliquary of Saint Louis of France. Beginning of fourteenth century. Slightly under life-size. Treasury, cathedral of Notre-Dame, Paris

Crown of Saint Louis (reigned as Louis IX of France from 1226 to 1270). c. 1260. The Louvre, Paris
▼

In the Early and High Middle Ages, goldsmith work ranked among the great creative arts, producing works of pure art as well as objects for church use. The costly materials employed were thought of as having in themselves a spiritual value, and when precious stones and pearls were used the object gained in symbolic significance. The goldsmith's art had much influence on both sculpture and manuscript illumination. However, with the ripening of the Gothic style, this relationship was inverted, and this type of art offered to the others less direct artistic impulses and, itself, took its inspiration from architecture and sculpture, whose ideas it reworked to its own ends. This meant that, little by little, it came to be relegated to the periphery of the major arts, to a craft whose place was among the applied arts. As a consequence, although its craftsmanly and artistic qualities remained high, it finally did little more than reflect, in its own exquisite way, ideas which had already been realized in other fields.

Nevertheless, even in Late Gothic times, the goldsmith's art was still capable, in its great achievements, of transforming the ideas and suggestions it borrowed into incredibly fine creations. This we see in the tower monstrances which resemble small architectural models of cathedrals and, like them, are soaring images of the Heavenly City. As a liturgical vessel for the consecrated hosts, the monstrance took its origin from the reliquaries which had been in use long before. It was only after the institution of the feast of Corpus Christi in 1264 that monstrances became common and, at the same time, much more elaborate: they were made larger, in order to be visible from far off, and were much more richly decorated in order to make them a fitting symbol of the Church. They are composed of a jointed pedestal and stem, like those of chalices, above which a cylindrical vessel for the host rests on a platform. Above the vessel a baldachin is supported by two buttressed piers, and on it, in the example seen here, stands a statuette of the Madonna which, in turn, is surmounted by another baldachin. Usually the spire is crowned by a cross as a reminder of the institution of the sacrament, the sacrificial death of Christ.

The theme of the Coronation of the Virgin does not occur in Byzantine art. It made its first appearance in England in the first half of the twelfth century and was taken up by the French Gothic around 1200, being used at first in the arch above a portal and in stained-glass windows.

In the last years of the thirteenth century, independent statues, as opposed to groups of figures, increased in importance. A single figure, or two closely related figures, made up a new form of devotional image intended to induce pious thoughts in the viewer. The new pietistic approach, which would reach its high point in the deeply emotional mysticism of the fourteenth century, thereby created a new artistic form which became a model for the entire last phase of the Middle Ages, one which served for private meditations and encouraged a personal, intimate relationship with the saints and sacred personages.

PARISIAN WORKSHOP. *Coronation of the Virgin.* End of thirteenth century. Painted and gilded ivory, $11 \times 9^7/_8''$. The Louvre, Paris

Resurrection, with the blessing ▶ Christ seated on His sarcophagus, in the arcades of which are seen the sleeping guards. c. 1290. Painted and gilded oak, $42^1/_2 \times 27^3/_4''$. Monastery of Wienhausen (near Hanover)

Christic and Saint John, from the Orphanage of Nazareth in Sigmaringen (Baden-Württemberg), probably the work of a sculptor from Constance. c. 1320. Painted and gilded oak, height 35″. State Museums, Berlin-Dahlem

The fusing of the two figures into a unity, the clasped hands, the complete surrender of the young saint as expressed in the closed eyes and the head resting on the shoulder of the Master, and Christ's meditative gaze which seems to contemplate more than the young disciple—all of these are related to the new concept of union with God as set forth in monastic contemplative writings, especially those of the Dominican and Franciscan women's orders, in this period of mysticism.

Vesper image, by a Middle Rhenish master. c. 1300. Painted limewood, height without base $10^{1}/_{2}''$. Rheinisches Landesmuseum, Bonn (formerly Roettgen Collection)

The German term *Vesperbild*—vesper image—derives from the contemplative prayers which refer in particular to the events which occurred after the Descent from the Cross, and it was German mysticism which conceived these devotional images as independent works of art. Apparently originating in the Franconian-Thuringian region, they spread throughout Germany to reach Italy, where they took the form of the *Pietà*. Their obvious realism serves to concentrate their emotional content and thereby to arouse sympathy for Mary and her dead Son.

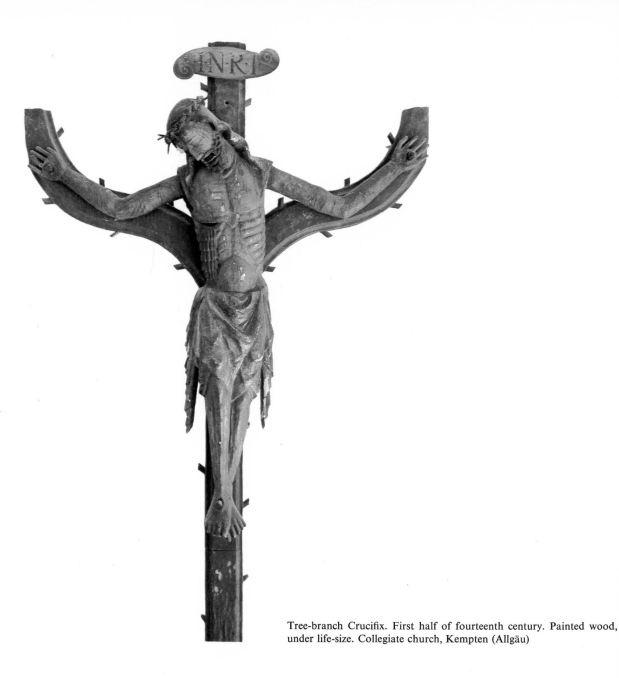

Tree-branch Crucifix. First half of fourteenth century. Painted wood, under life-size. Collegiate church, Kempten (Allgäu)

The art of the early fourteenth century was impregnated with mysticism. It portrayed the sufferings of Christ with a merciless realism designed to arouse deep compassion. The body in the agony of death is disfigured to the point of ugliness. In the same way, the literature of the time entered into the most gruesome details. Here, the Cross in the form of a tree branch is an allusion to the *arbor vitae*, the tree of life, and it makes of the crucified Christ a visual symbol of the vast context of Redemption. It was in those years that Europe was being ravaged by the plague, and men were so much the more readily touched by depictions of suffering.

Crucifix (detail). First half of fourteenth century.
Wood, under life-size. Cathedral, Perpignan

Tomb of Archbishop Friedrich von Hohenlohe (d. 1352) (detail). Middle of fourteenth century. Stone, originally painted. Bamberg Cathedral

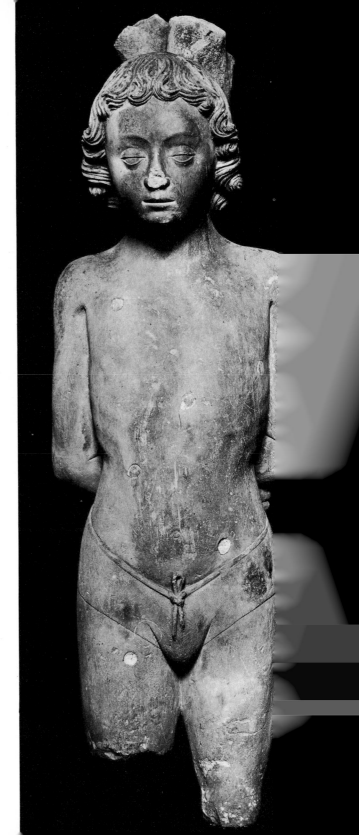

As we have seen already with the blessing Christ of Wienhausen and the Christ with Saint John from Sigmaringen, the mysticism of the time embraced images of consolation also. More than ever before, religious images were directly related to private devotions. They were not only associated with specific religious texts but were conceived to encourage the faithful to direct communion with God. From this arose the emotional over-emphasis which was intended to arouse similar emotions in the beholder.

In tomb sculpture in which the deceased was portrayed in effigy with some attempt at portraiture, fourteenth-century mysticism turned away from the delight in human appearance of the previous century. Here the figure bends in an unstatic curve, the body under the garments is scarcely sensed, the face shows the emaciated but transfigured traits of an ascetic. In the statue of Saint Sebastian, he is depicted as a weak youth fated to succumb to his adversaries, but his face expresses the peace and bliss found in martyrdom. The youthful body of the saint is portrayed with a delicacy designed to stir the viewer to greater compassion. Religious art here becomes touched with eroticism, just as in contemporary devotional literature, especially the visions of the Heavenly Bridegroom written down by nuns. Secular love poetry had its roots in the same sublimation of feeling (see page 113).

Saint Sebastian, by a French sculptor. Middle of fourteenth century. Stone. The Louvre, Paris ▶

Mirror case with lovers and esquire, by a Parisian ▶
workshop. c. 1320–30. Ivory relief, diameter 4″.
Collection Kofler-Truniger, Lucerne

Luxuria (Lust), by a Franco-Flemish workshop.
c. 1320–30. Oak relief, 57½×24⅜″. State Museums, Berlin-Dahlem

The sculpture portrait of Saint Louis (King of France from
1226 to 1270) with his consort (died 1295) demonstrates the
smooth transition between religious and secular mysticism.
In secular terms, the tender embrace refers to the fact that
Margaret accompanied her husband on his crusade to the
Holy Land in 1248. However, the statue was made for
religious purposes, commissioned for the altar of Saint
Lawrence in the château of the author of the Chronicles of
Saint Louis, Jean de Joinville. It is not impossible that the
sculptor may have known his subjects in person, because his
statue has certain authentic features. It is known, for example, that on his crusade the King let his beard grow (compare the reliquary bust on page 100). In his right hand he
holds an architectural structure often depicted at that time,
a symbol of the rotunda over the tomb of Christ in Jerusalem,
whose reconquest was the goal of the Crusaders. The Queen
apparently once held a lily, the emblem of French sovereignty.

The sculptor clearly differentiated his male and female figures according to the spiritual conceptions of the Middle Ages. The King stands erect, both feet firmly planted on the earth, his gaze directed afar on the task he had set himself. The Queen, in contrast, clings to her husband, according to the Biblical injunction, and sees only him, for his care is her task in life. Her smile recalls that of the allegorical figure of Lust on the page opposite: to the medieval mind a woman's smile was the visible sign of her womanly perfection, expressing both her spirituality and her delight in the things of the world.

Saint Louis with his wife Margaret of Provence, by a Strasbourg master. End of thirteenth or beginning of fourteenth century. Oak. State Museums, Berlin-Dahlem (on loan)

The manuscript assembled by Rüdiger Manesse (died 1304), a town councilor of Zurich, and his son Johannes (died 1297), which was later embellished with 138 full-page miniatures, is the most precious collection of Minnesinger poems known. The poems are impregnated with the spirit of the age of mysticism, aristocratic and worldly but, at the same time, spiritual in content. This love poetry is by no means a naïve expression of spontaneous feeling. Rather, its poetic images and formulas belong to a highly formalized court tradition. The poet and his lady play their roles according to rigorous conventions which were transmitted from Arabic Spain to Provence, where they were given a highly artistic formulation. The hero and lover must always assume the role of humble servitor to his lady, even if he be a great sovereign. He aspires with longing and veneration to the love of an unattainable great queen, places his life at her service, but never attains the fulfillment of his desires. His love concerns only himself, never his beloved. She is only the pretext for his poetizing, an ideal woman remote from all earthly concerns. For all its unreality, the troubadours and minnesingers adhered to the rules of the game with passion and tenderness, with spirit and art.

View of Prague showing the Charles Bridge, Hradčany Castle, and the cathedral of Saint Vitus. The cathedral was begun by Mathieu d'Arras in 1344, continued by Peter Parler in 1353, and not fully completed until the twentieth century. The bridge was begun by Peter Parler in 1357 and completed in the fifteenth century

Interior of the cathedral of Saint Vitus, Prague, showing the clerestory and triforium of the south side of the nave. After 1350

PETER PARLER (active 1330 –78). *Portrait Bust of Emperor Charles IV.* 1375–93. Lower triforium, Prague Cathedral

Under Charles IV, the Imperial court of Prague became a leading artistic center, and new artistic impulses spread from it throughout Europe. In contrast to the mysticism of the first half of the fourteenth century, after the middle of the century there was a decisive return to the High Gothic principles of the preceding century. A striking example of this is the cathedral which the Emperor had built in imitation of the French cathedrals. It was begun by Mathieu d'Arras in 1344, and after his death in 1352, a German architect and sculptor from Schwäbisch Gmünd, Peter Parler, carried it forward on his own plans. His new conception of a solid corporeality which aimed at an impression of definable space was opposed to the mannered, excessively detailed, unsculptural figures of medieval mysticism. This is apparent in his architecture and sculpture alike, in the spatially soaring disposition of the walls of the cathedral as well as in the portrait busts lining the triforium. In the latter, there is a new and clearer naturalism with emphasis on physical volumes and on individual, personal traits.

Karlštejn Castle, near Prague. 1348–57

Chapel of the Holy Cross, Karlštejn Castle. Decorated
c. 1365

Near Prague, in the Bohemian forests, Charles IV built Karlštejn, a castle hidden away and difficult of access, set high on an easily defended rock surrounded by valleys. There the King kept the royal treasures, and there too was his refuge in the event of flight from the capital. A tall tower rising above the other buildings contained the royal apartments, and to it the monarch could retreat if the castle were attacked. The decoration of the Chapel of the Holy Cross still survives in good state, and has a sumptuousness recalling Byzantine and Oriental interiors. Deep, gilded depressed Gothic arches frame walls which are entirely covered with pictures. The richly ornamental gilded base of the walls is studded with thousands of fragments of varicolored marble and agate, which seem to be placed haphazardly but, in fact, are grouped to form crosses. Italian and Central European artists were responsible for the decoration. Tommaso da Modena and his follower Theoderic of Prague, whose *Crucifixion* crowns the wall above the tabernacle, created here a new style which was soon to spread to the West.

In Prague in 1349, Charles IV founded a painters' guild organized after the model of the builders' corporations. Their school made an essential contribution to the development of panel painting which, from the fourteenth century on, played an ever more important part in the creation of altarpieces. In contrast to the broad surfaces of wall painting, the smaller dimensions of the panel quickly led to quite different principles of composition and to an imaginative use of color, which intensified both the expressive character of the picture and its life-likeness. Increasingly, religious art profited from the techniques of a whole newly discovered world of art: landscape, vegetation, the placing of figures in space, the greater verisimilitude of portraits were all new acquisitions which were incorporated into religious pictures.

MASTER OF THE CYCLE OF
VYŠŠI BROD (HOHENFURT).
Nativity. After 1350. Tempera on panel, $33^5/_8 \times 37^3/_8''$.
National Gallery, Prague

MASTER OF TŘEBOŇ (WIT- ▶
TINGAU). *Resurrection of
Christ*. c. 1380. Tempera on
panel, $53 \times 36^1/_2''$. National
Gallery, Prague

Comparison between two Bohemian painters makes the development clear. With the Master of Vyšši Brod
there is a synthesis of traditional French Gothic and Byzantine elements, though with a new feeling for
organization in which each detail is given a clear rhythm within a strophic grouping. On the other hand,
the Třeboň Master's thinking transcends the figures as such and proceeds not from details but from
the over-all organization: pictorial space and pictorial image are one. The forms are not laid out in
juxtaposition but interpenetrate and are intensified to become something visionary. Before a deep dark
space, Christ rises up above His still-sealed sarcophagus, a closed form in the dark red of His mantle.

Master Theoderic of Prague has his place between the two artists we have just seen and who represent the chief phases of the development. After the Byzantine and Gothic links as seen in the work of the Vyšší Brod Master, with Theoderic Italian influences entered into Bohemian painting. The lesson of Giotto was learned in Prague from the example of Tommaso da Modena, but it was transformed by the artist's own personality and by the new conception of physical volumes which had prevailed since Parler. In the powerfully foursquare portrayal of a Father of the Church, a painterly, concentrated, broad massiveness of form is what is responsible for the effect. No longer is there a linear outlining of the figure as earlier. The body of the Saint spreads out to the frame of the picture and even breaks through it. The strongly expressive unity of color contributes to the concentration of the image and becomes an attribute of the personage depicted.

MASTER THEODERIC OF PRAGUE (documented 1359–69). *Saint Augustine*, from a cycle of the Church Fathers in the chapel of the Holy Cross, Karlštejn Castle. 1359–69. Tempera with gilding on panel, $44^1/_2 \times 40^1/_2''$. National Gallery, Prague

Apse of the Holy Cross Minster, Schwäbisch Gmünd. Begun as a hall church by Heinrich Parler in 1351. The three-sided closing of the nave matches up with the seven-sided ambulatory of the choir as seen from the outside

The hall churches, as developed in southern Germany in particular, under the influence of the Parler family, were responsible for a thoroughgoing change in the basic structure of Gothic churches of the time. Even from the outside one can see how the new conception differs from that of the previous cathedrals. The structure appears as a unified, compact mass, no longer broken up by flying buttresses and no longer having a high nave towering above the aisles. A common roof, rising steeply to its apex, covers both nave and aisles, all of which are of the same height. The exterior of the choir is divided horizontally into two zones of the same height which are separated by a heavy cornice. The new system of construction made it feasible to reduce the buttressing to simple projections placed flat against the walls, and this emphasizes the solid character of the uninterrupted wall.

View of the nave, Sankt Martin, Landshut. Choir begun before 1392 by Hans von Burghausen (d. 1432); nave begun before 1407, continued after the architect's death by, presumably, Hans Stethaimer

◀ View of the choir ambulatory, Sankt Lorenz, Nuremberg. Choir begun in 1439 by Konrad Heinzelmann (c. 1390 –1454) in imitation of the choir in Schwäbisch Gmünd, design modified after 1454 by Konrad Roritzer (c. 1410 –75), completed in 1477

The interior of a hall church is unified differently from that of a basilica-type cathedral. The nave is no longer emphatically separated from the aisles, and the same piers support the vaultings of all of them. In the late phase the piers rise directly to the vaults without capitals, so that the earlier distinction between weight-bearing and thrust-bearing members is abandoned. The aisles are prolonged to make an ambulatory encircling the choir. As a consequence, the rigorous emphasis on the east-west orientation of the interior is relaxed. Impressive transverse relations result from this, and the effect of soaring upward in space, aimed at in earlier churches, is transformed into an optical impression of circular space.

As can be seen in Sankt Lorenz, Nuremberg, the uniform height of all the vaults brought about new static relationships in the hall churches. Extreme measures were no longer required to support the thrust and strain on the exterior of the building, because the vaults maintain an evenly distributed equilibrium more readily than in the basilica-type cathedrals.

In Sankt Martin, Landshut (facing page), we have a long hall without transept, with slender, very tall piers ($70 \times 3'$) in the nave and, at the sides, nichelike chapels which enliven the walls. On the exterior of this church there is an epitaph of the architect with his portrait (see page 217).

AMBROGIO LORENZETTI (documented 1319–c. 1348). *View of an Imaginary City*. c. 1338–40. Tempera on panel, 13 × 8⅝″. Pinacoteca, Siena

RODOLFO GUARIENTO (active 1338–65). *Angel with Demon Enchained*. Tempera on panel, 35³/₈ × 22⁷/₈″. Museo Civico, Padua

We know something about Ambrogio Lorenzetti's activities in Siena between 1324 and 1345. His fresco cycle in the Palazzo Pubblico of that city, an *Allegory of Good and Bad Government*, has led some writers to see in him the first Humanist artist of modern times. In this picture of an imaginary city, Gothic constructivism is combined with a conception of space which is virtually an anticipation of that of the Renaissance, not only in its attempt to master perspective but also, almost more, by virtue of the gifts of observation of the artist. He has looked at his subject with utter objectivity and then, with the aid of geometry, sought to set down what he has seen. This innovation is so much the more striking by contrast with the Paduan Guariento's Angel. Guariento clung to the Gothic style as conceived by Giotto, and did not seek to go beyond its limits. This is apparent in the figure's severe and sober pose, as well as in the expressive, strong coloring.

The commune of Siena in the Middle Ages was dedicated to the Mother of God as protectress of the city. The Madonna crowned the city gates, appeared on the city seal. In the council hall of the communal palace, political deliberations took place beneath a fresco in which the heavenly council of those saints who were especially venerated in the city is assembled around the throne of the Madonna. The sensitive interrelation of all details in a Gothic beauty of line suggests that Simone may have been influenced by French miniature painting.

Even in the fifteenth century, when the other centers of Italy had accepted the Early Renaissance and were penetrating deeper and deeper into the means of depicting reality, Siena remained faithful to the tradition dominant there ever since Simone Martini. Its rejection of realism was bound up with a deep current of mysticism which, in its painting, led to an almost surrealistic fantasy. Long after other schools, Siena continued to use gold backgrounds and to reject modeling of figures after nature. Moreover, the small format was preferred, along with a miniature-like way of painting. It was Sassetta and Giovanni di Paolo who expressed most clearly the essence of Sienese art. Sassetta's *Mystic Marriage of Saint Francis* illustrates a parable of Saint Bonaventura which tells how Chastity, Humility, and Poverty appeared to the Saint who took Poverty as his bride. Two events are presented simultaneously: the marriage and the return to Heaven of the three sisters, with Poverty looking back at her spiritual husband. The scene of the legend, Mount Amiata, is clearly defined.

GIOVANNI DI PAOLO
(c. 1403–82). *Expulsion
from Paradise.* 1445. Tempera on panel, 17³/₄ ×
20¹/₂″. Lehman Collection, New York

STEFANO DI GIOVANNI ▶
SASSETTA (c. 1400–50).
*The Mystic Marriage of
Saint Francis of Assisi.*
1437–44. Tempera on
panel, 34⁵/₈ × 20⁵/₈″.
Musée Condé, Chantilly

While this Madonna as a whole is in the International Gothic style of the early fifteenth century, and the drapery still has the characteristic Gothic folds, the emphasis on the clear forms of the head reflects the new ideal of beauty which was introduced in the Early Renaissance.

WORKSHOP OF NINO PISANO (active 1349– c. 1368). *Madonna*, from an *Annunciation* (detail). Wood, height of full figure 5′ 11¹/₂″. The Louvre, Paris

One of the most significant themes in the practical theology of the Middle Ages was the fear of Hell. In the *Divine Comedy*, which Dante began around 1311, Hell is described in terrifying detail, but even before then the sculptors who worked on the great cathedrals had shown the horrors awaiting the damned on Judgment Day. The depiction of infernal atrocities seemed one of the surest means of convincing a self-centered humanity of the ideal goals of the Church. In fifteenth-century painting the theme was depicted with even more painstaking detail than in cathedral sculpture, and it even instilled a medieval spirit into Renaissance art, as Signorelli's frescoes demonstrate. Signorelli's nudes are imbued with movement, modeled almost too sharply by light and shadow. They attest to a complete mastery of the means of depicting the human organism in motion and of a clear definition of the overlappings and foreshortenings of the nude bodies. All this is Humanistic in orientation, and yet the denigration of physical beauty, the emphasis on human emotions and on the bizarre nature of the demoniac creatures, show how opposed to the new Renaissance conceptions were such depictions with their disdain for earthly pride. Here, then, we see two ages in collision.

ENGUERRAND CHARONTON (also known as QUARTON) (c. 1410–c. 1466). *Hell*, detail from the altarpiece of the *Coronation of the Virgin*. 1453–54. Tempera on panel. Hospice, Villeneuve-lès-Avignon.

LUCA SIGNORELLI (c. 1450–1523). *The Damned Cast into Hell* (detail). 1499–1500. Fresco. Chapel of San Brizio, cathedral of Orvieto

On the Well of Moses, which unfortunately survives in fragments only, the statues of the prophets are so individualized as to seem portraits. Its vast iconographical program is remarkable: above the water of the Fount of Life, Old Testament patriarchs bear a Mount of Calvary crowned by a crucifix (now lost) as a symbol of the Redemption proclaimed by the New Testament.

▲
CLAUS SLUTER (active c. 1385–1406). Angel and Prophets, detail ▶ of the Well of Moses. 1395–1405. Polychromed and gilded stone, full figures c. 6′ high. Chartreuse of Champmol, Dijon

The painter of the fresco on the facing page, apparently from Prague, was clearly influenced by the scenes of nature in the Papal Palace at Avignon (see page 38), but by means of the graduated size of the figures and the dark-blue background shimmering through trees and plants, he created an atmosphere with a truer sense of landscape and space.

Spring, from a cycle of the Seasons by a Bohemian artist (detail). Beginning of fifteenth century. Fresco. Castello del Buon Consiglio, Trent

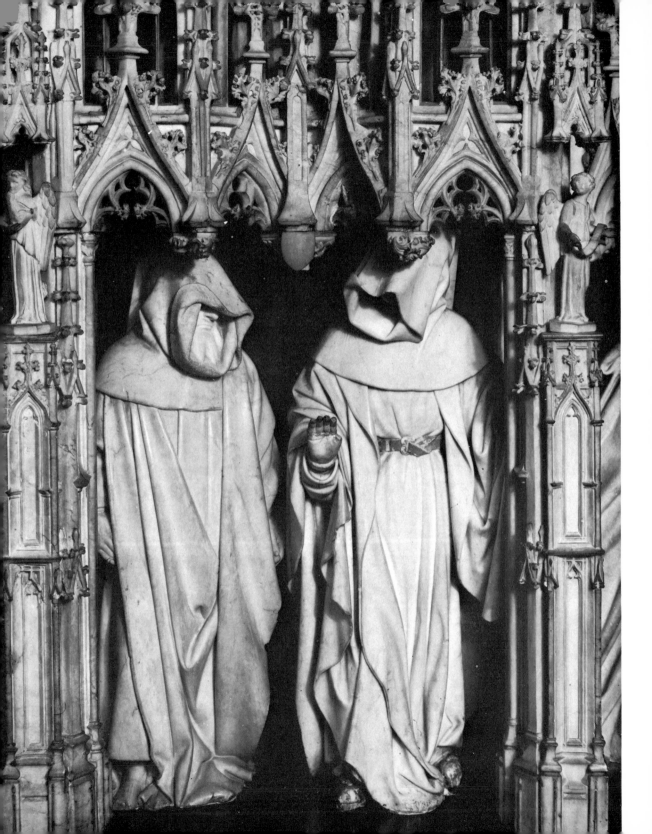

Claus Sluter, of Haarlem in Holland, was the foremost sculptor of the period around 1400. His chief works were done for the court of Burgundy. In his tomb for Philip the Bold he created a new iconographical tradition which continued in tomb sculpture until the end of the fifteenth century: freestanding statues of monks, their faces partly hidden under their hoods, attend the bier weeping—whence their name of *pleurants*.

Weeping monks *(pleurants)* from the architectural frieze on the tomb of Jean sans Peur and Margaret of Bavaria, now in the Musée des Beaux-Arts, Dijon. Begun 1443 by JUAN DE LA HUERTA (d. c. 1462) and completed by 1470 by ANTOINE LE MOITURIER (c. 1425–c. 1494). Alabaster, height $15^3/_8$ to $16^1/_8$''. The *pleurants* were done in imitation of those on the tomb of Philippe le Hardi which was begun around 1384 by JEAN DE MARVILLE, continued by CLAUS SLUTER in 1404, and completed in 1410 by HENNEQUIN DE PRINDALE and CLAUS DE WERVE

ANTOINE LE MOITURIER (c. 1425–c. 1494), attributed. Tomb of Philippe Pot. 1477–83. Polychromed stone, 5' 11'' × 8' 8''. The Louvre, Paris

Madonna and Child, by a Burgundian sculptor. c. 1410–20. Stone, c. $31\frac{1}{2}''$ high. The Louvre, Paris

Claus Sluter played an essential part in the development of a style which dominated art throughout Europe around 1400 and is called, therefore, the International Gothic. Close relations between Burgundy and Bohemia, and between Bohemia and southern Germany, account for the diffusion of the so-called "Beautiful Madonnas," which are among the finest products of the style (see page 160). Characteristic of such works in Burgundy is the gentle framing of the figure by drapery. This we saw already in the weeping monks; to the Madonnas it lends a tender loveliness of expression while, at the same time, emphasizing the closed volumes of the entire statue.

Hôtel-Dieu, Beaune (Burgundy), built 1443–51 by JEHAN WISCRÈRE at the expense of Nicolas Rolin, Chancellor of Burgundy, as a free charity hospital

This Gothic hospital, still functioning today, combines Burgundian and Flemish architectural features such as oak half-timbering, lead ornaments on the gables, and glazed tiles on the roofs. The nuns who staffed it came from Malines, and the covered porch running along the building permitted them to get about in bad weather and reach the sickrooms which are accessible only from the exterior. The hospital is among the best preserved examples of medieval secular architecture. Its finely designed structure and the costly carpentry-work lavished on an almshouse reflect credit on the wealthy, aristocratic benefactor who, in accord with the medieval belief in the sanctity of good deeds, gave practical form to a work of mercy.

The Sibyl Agrippa, on the tomb of Philibert the Handsome, Saint-Nicolas, Brou (Eure-et-Loir). Franco-Flemish. 1516–22. Marble

Eve. By a French sculptor. Fifteenth century. Present whereabouts unknown

Head of Saint Fortunade. By a French sculptor. c. 1450–60. Marble, under life-size. Church of Sainte-Fortunade (Corrèze)

The French sculptors of the fifteenth century achieved a special, almost tender sentiment in their female figures, much like that of the International Gothic style in Burgundy, in whose Madonnas loveliness became almost a formula. This led in time to the natural grace of the dreamy maidens on the tomb in Brou who represent the sibyls.

In this miniature (left), a wall separates the Garden from the mountains and the ocean. Inside, under a monstrance-like baldachin, is the Fountain of Life. In the right foreground, God unites in marriage Adam and Eve and warns them against transgressing His commandments. At the left, Eve is tempted to taste of the Tree of Knowledge by the serpent in woman's form, and in the foreground Eve leads Adam into sin. At the right they are expelled from Paradise through a golden Gothic portal.

As early as the start of the fifteenth century, a marked difference appears between the painting of the Early Renaissance in Italy and that of the Late Gothic in the Netherlands, though influences flowed in both directions. The Burgundian territory was both a kind of catch basin and a center of diffusion for all the new conceptions of painting. It had close ties with Flanders, Paris, Prague, and, through Avignon, with the courts of Italy. Miniature painting played a particularly important part in the development of a realistic concept of nature, and this was fostered by the medieval philosophical theory as to the reality of ideas. The small format, and the fact that commissions came from enlightened private individuals, permitted artists to experiment in the depiction of nature, and their conquests in the field of manuscript illumination were rapidly taken up and exploited in the larger forms of panel painting. Broederlam's altarpiece shows how the traditional formulas for depicting landscape, which had been inherited from the Byzantines, gradually came to absorb the more modern conception in which space and landscape were considered as a unity.

While religious art continued to be more dependent on traditional notions, constrained as it was to accept the primacy of ideas as opposed to reality, secular art quickly came closer to a realistic attitude toward the visible world. For the first time, miniaturists were commissioned to illustrate nonreligious books, whose subject matter was drawn from men's notions of the universe. In the Book of Hours of the Duke of Berry, the miniatures make up a calendar in which the daily activities of men are shown in association with the course of the seasons and planets as set into motion by God. For all the cosmic significance of these miniatures, here for the first time appears the Flemish delight in narration, the native feeling for real things, for landscape, for the work that men do in their daily lives, and for architecture as a distinctive part of a city or landscape.

Departure for the Forest, miniature from the *Livre de la Chasse* of Gaston Phébus. c. 1405–10. Ms. fr. 616, Bibliothèque Nationale, Paris

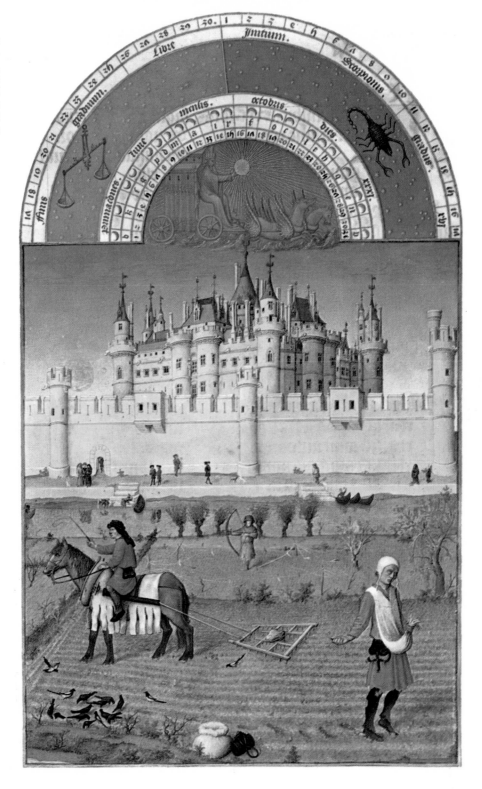

THE LIMBOURG BROTHERS. *October*, in *Les Très Riches Heures du Duc de Berry*. 1413–16. Miniature. Musée Condé, Chantilly. Peasants work the fields while citizens stroll along the banks of the Seine in front of the medieval castle of the Louvre in Paris

Vanitas: Allegory of the Transitoriness of Life, by a French ▶ sculptor. c. 1450. Ivory, height 5³/₄″. Bayerisches National-museum, Munich

As men turned more and more to the things of this world in the Late Middle Ages, they were also forcibly reminded that at the end lies death, *memento mori*, that man is mortal and all his earthly goods are of no avail. To understand just how seriously this warning was meant, it is enough to recall the wars and plagues which ravaged Europe in the fourteenth and fifteenth centuries and which could snuff out human life in a night. Literature and art explored every aspect of the theme of the transitoriness of life. Everyone read the *Ars moriendi*, an instructive book, often illustrated with woodcuts, on "the art of dying in a state of grace," in which was recounted how Hell and Heaven struggle for the dying man's soul, how the dying man should commend his soul to God, and, as the final illustration in the book, how to die a happy death in God. It was not only in books that the lesson was preached. This tiny ivory statuette strips away the seductions of earthly existence: Death brandishes the Cross as an admonition before the tender body of a young girl.

147

MASTER OF THE TRIUMPH OF DEATH (FRANCESCO TRAINI?). *The Quick and the Dead*, detail of the cycle *The Triumph of Death*. c. 1360. Fresco. Campo Santo, Pisa

In Triumphs and Dances of Death, the Late Middle Ages gave symbolic expression to the inevitability of death, a reminder that only by accepting death's certainty can man endure its horrors. Every man must die once, and Death comes to all alike, whatever rank they may hold in life—these were the highly instructive principles of these depictions which showed the inexorable round in which Death led all mankind. Often such pictures were accompanied by dialogued inscriptions with pleas for mercy and refusals. Among the most famous of such representations of the Dance of Death in the Late Middle Ages are those in La Chaise-Dieu, Basel, and Lübeck, and their tradition was perpetuated into the sixteenth century in woodcuts by Holbein and others.

Dance of Death. c. 1450–70. Fresco, height 55″. North side of cloister, abbey church, La Chaise-Dieu (Haute-Loire). Drawing of frieze after Gonse. Facing page: detail of the original fresco

SOUTHERN FRENCH MASTER. *Pietà*, from Villeneuve-lès-Avignon. Before 1457. Oil and tempera on panel, 63³/₄ × 86″. The Louvre, Paris

MASTER OF THE HOURS OF ROHAN. *Pietà*, in the *Livre d'Heures de Rohan*

In the expressive art of the Late Gothic, symbols of death were given a powerfully emotive form in which the accent was placed on the lamentation of the living. In French painting, this appears with the theme of the *Pietà*, of Mary's mourning over the dead Christ. In contrast to the fourteenth century, when this theme first became prominent, the artist no longer strove to arouse the emotions of the viewer by means of the martyred body of Christ, but instead concentrates the entire attention on Mary's sorrow. The body of Christ is dead, drained, a cast-off mortal shell, rigid and immobile as when it was taken down from the Cross; Mary is frozen in uncomprehending grief. Despite certain influences from the Netherlands, this painting grew out of the tradition of Simone Martini and remains bound to the abstractionist tendencies of the Sienese Gothic in its use of the gold background, large haloes, and the emphatic poses and gestures of the figures.

As never before, fifteenth-century piety was concerned with the lives and legends of the saints, and the saints began to play an ever more important role as personal intercessors. All social classes alike venerated them. Where facts failed, legend and imagination supplied the want, and painters exercised their highly inventive fancy in depicting events from the saints' lives as if they had just occurred among people of the contemporary world. Not only the clothing worn but even the events portrayed tell us much about the practices of the times, as in the precise rendering of the gruesome torture to which the saintly maiden Apollonia was subjected, bound to a board, her hair pulled out, her teeth ripped out of her mouth by long iron pincers. Seemingly irreconcilable incidents were concentrated into a single image in order to make the narration even more convincingly impressive. (The miniature below depicts a scene from a Mystery play.)

JEAN FOUQUET (c. 1420–after 1477). *Martyrdom of Saint Apollonia*, in the *Livre d'Heures d'Étienne Chevalier*. c. 1452–60. Miniature, $6^1/_2 \times 4^3/_4''$. Musée Condé, Chantilly

Coat of arms of the Duke of Berry, held by two angels. Fifteenth century. Section of a stained-glass window, Bourges Cathedral

The painstaking precision of manuscript illumination, which is more like goldsmiths' work than painting, became a model for other arts, even for finely worked tapestries and stained-glass windows. Not only the new realism but also the attention to the finest details set a new standard for art. Thus, painters of stained glass no longer worked only with bits of colored glass held together by lead mounting, but now coated the glass with black lead and then carefully scraped it away to model in clear glass the faces and garments of the figures.

Une nupt en ce mois passe
Trauaille tourmente lasse
fforment pensez ou lit me mis
Comme homme las qui A si mis
Son cueur en la mercy damours
Que ma bie en plains et en plours

The conviction that all sensual delights were merely transitory led not only to their mortification but also to their intensification, to an unconcerned and hearty play with eroticism. The nude was portrayed as an object delightful in itself, with no need of some theological allegory as an excuse, and so we find it in a baker's mold or in the coat of arms of a learned university rector. The polarity between sheer joy in life and asceticism was, in fact, one of the decisive factors in the Late Middle Ages' attitude toward existence.

The Judgment of Paris. Rhenish work, middle of fifteenth century. Terra-cotta gingerbread mold, diameter c. 6³/₈″. Schweizerisches Landesmuseum, Zurich

Coat of arms of Hieronymus von Weyblingen, Rector of the university of Basel, from the first volume of the matriculation register of the university. 1485. Vellum, 11¹/₄ × 8¹/₁₆″. University Library, Basel

The Horsemen of the Apocalypse, from a cycle of tapestries on the Revelation of Saint John, designed by Hennequin of Bruges and executed by Nicolas Bataille, formerly in the cathedral of Angers. After 1377–81. Museum, Angers

King David, figure on a choir stall. After 1350. Wood, height c. 11³/₄″. Bamberg Cathedral

To the rhythm of the nature-oriented, ascetic-mystical currents of the time, the International Gothic style of around 1400 brought a special accent. This style, known in Germany as the "soft style," substituted a new lyrical mysticism for the way the human body had been depicted in the time of the Parlers, and itself was supplanted around 1430 by a "hard" or "angular" style. One of the earliest examples of this new approach is the epical cycle of tapestries in Angers in which the Revelation of Saint John was given a poetic, visionary embodiment in art. The gruesome realism of the event, the avenging horsemen galloping ruthlessly over a prostrate humanity, is ennobled by the unworldly coloring and by a setting concentrated down to essentials. From a Gothic edifice at the side, the Saint himself looks out contemplatively on the terrible scene unrolling before him.

So-called "Beautiful Madonna," from Český Krumlov, Bohemia. c. 1400. Limestone with traces of old polychrome, height 44¹/₈". Kunsthistorisches Museum, Vienna

Bohemia, Silesia, the Salzburg and Upper Bavarian regions produced masterworks of sculpture in the International Gothic style. These have been designated as "Beautiful Madonnas" because of their graceful elegance and the soft draperies which flow smoothly without sharp breaks in line. The childlike charm of these lovely statues is further emphasized by their small dimensions. The draperies playing around the figures have virtually a life of their own, with a contrapuntal complexity of great expressivity. Lines of draperies rising steeply are answered by plunging cascades of folds, though all lines are rigorously organized into variations on the motif of the triangle. Similarly, the rounded curves of the folds are played off against effects of depth in the drapery. The upper bodies of the Mother and Child bend in opposite directions, but the contrast is then resolved by the opposite inclination of the head of the Madonna as she looks down at the Infant. There is another contrast: the graceful loveliness of the figures is always tempered by an execution which is forcefully and rigorously organized.

"Beautiful Madonna," from Seeon
am Chiemsee. c. 1430. Polychromed
and gilded wood, $42\frac{1}{2} \times 33\frac{1}{8}$".
Bayerisches Nationalmuseum,
Munich

UPPER RHENISH MASTER. *Garden of Paradise*. c. 1410. Tempera and gilding on panel, 10³/₈ × 13¹/₈″. Städelsches Kunstinstitut, Frankfurt am Main (on loan from the Historical Museum)

The purest expression of the International Gothic style can be found in this *Garden of Paradise*. In it, medieval symbolism combines in the most gracious manner with an entirely new feeling for reality, with an awakening interest in real objects and in the things of nature. Mary sits among her companions in a walled garden which, itself, is one of her symbols, the *Hortus conclusus* of the Song of Songs. For the first time in German painting a blue sky gleams brightly beyond this wall of Paradise, and there are trees with birds fluttering back and forth across the wall. The garden is watered by the Fount of Life, and there is the Tree of Life together with eighteen species of plants which are defined with botanical precision: both flowers and healing herbs, a veritable medicinal herbarium. Mary is intent on her book, Saint Dorothy gathers cherries, Martha draws water from the well, and Saint Cecilia permits the Infant Jesus to strum on her harp. At the right, an archangel and two saintly knights look on: Michael with the ape-devil enchained, George with the dragon he vanquished, and Sebastian. Even if we do not completely grasp the symbolism of the presence of all these personages, who were probably included on the orders of the donor, the picture itself speaks to us by means of its jewel-like colors, by the unconcealed delight of the artist in the intimacy of this peaceful company, by the way the many precisely formed details have been brought lovingly together in a harmony undisturbed by any hint of dissonance.

Pietà, from the Monastery of Seeon am Chiemsee. 1420–25. Polychromed stone, height 29$^{1}/_{2}$″. Bayerisches National-museum, Munich

Even grief is lent a special grace in the International Gothic style. The body of this dead Christ is exaggeratedly long as it lies across the lap of the almost childlike Mother, who supports the head with her hand. Realism is not the aim here. The overlarge dead body and the excessively elongated arm of Mary both serve to intensify the expression of mourning—a burden too great for the Mother's fragile weakness. The vesper image of medieval mysticism returns here, but the lamentation is transformed into something lyrical.

164

MIDDLE RHENISH MASTER. *Pietà*, from Oestrich. c. 1420. Polychromed and gilded walnut, height 34⁵/₈″. Liebighaus, Frankfurt am Main

In contrast to the gentle art of the South German masters, the vesper images of the Rhineland remained more closely attached to the mystical tradition of the fourteenth century, and it was in those regions that the suffering Christ had been portrayed with stark realism. The desiccated body, stiff in the rigor of death, is more tightly linked with the figure of Mary, seems so much more her son, and the legs fall across the downward-plunging folds of her mantle which themselves are as much an expression of the Mother's contained grief as are the features of her face.

MASTER BERTRAM OF MINDEN (c. 1345–1415). *The Third Day of Creation: Creation of the Plants*, from the Grabow Altarpiece, formerly on the high altar of the Petrikirche, Hamburg. 1379. Tempera and gilding on panel, 33$^1/_8$ × 22$^1/_4$″. Kunsthalle, Hamburg

Saint Bartholomew, from a group of twelve Apostles. c. 1400. Terra cotta, originally painted, 25$^5/_8$ × 24″. Germanisches Nationalmuseum, Nuremberg

The figure of Saint Bartholomew (left) is a major example of the International Gothic style as practiced in Nuremberg, with massive rendering of the body and a dense flow of drapery. Although sculptors had previously made small models in terra cotta, in Nuremberg these became statues in their own right. For the first time since the sculpture at Bamberg and Naumburg, artists aimed at characterization. The small format and the easily modeled material made it possible to portray the passionate character of the subject, as shown in the large head, furrowed brow, agitatedly coiling hair, the crossed legs, and the hand firmly leafing through the book.

The altarpiece by Master Bertram played a significant role in the development of landscape painting. While the *Garden of Paradise* (page 163) and Stefan Lochner's closely related *Madonna in the Rose Garden* (page 168) are both set in a closed, idyllic space, Bertram's altarpiece went far beyond them, although it was done earlier. This fragment of landscape, a stage prop to symbolize the third day of Creation, has more coherence than many landscapes done later. The entire setting is taken in at a glance. It is not overpowered by its details, and the dark shadows of the forest convince us that the artist has observed them in life. What is more, Bertram shows his mastery in the sculpturesque power with which the Creator is poised against the infinite space of the gold background, in the impressiveness of the gesture of creation, and in the clear distinction between the Creator and His creation. Here one can trace influences from Giotto by way of the Bohemian school, which may perhaps have transmitted them directly.

"The painter Hubert van Eyck, whom no one excelled, began the work, Jan who was second in art completed it . . . in the year of 1432 on the 16th of May." So reads the proud inscription on the great altarpiece in Ghent. What is certain is that the work and its authors ushered in a new epoch in Western painting which led, without interruption, from the Late Middle Ages to modern times. In the lower central panel is seen the Adoration of the Mystic Lamb. To the altar set in an open landscape, pilgrims stream in from all sides, in a procession which carries over from the side wings. Above is God the Father, flanked by Mary and John, musician angels, and, at the outer extremities, Adam and Eve. Although it seems to be composed of separate pictures, the altarpiece has an indisputable over-all unity, even though close and far views still alternate. With almost inexplicable sureness, the individual areas of color are subordinated to a total coloristic plan. Every detail is rendered with utmost precision, and this Adam and Eve may be regarded as the first nudes to be true to nature in all of Western painting. A new vision and a new way of transposing into paint what is seen create, in this work, a new unity out of a diversity of elements.

STEFAN LOCHNER (active 1410–51). *The Madonna in the Rose Garden.* c. 1440. Tempera and gilding on oak panel, 19⁷/₈ × 15³/₄". Wallraf Richartz Museum, Cologne

HUBERT (d. 1426) and JAN (c. 1390–1441) VAN EYCK. The Ghent Altarpiece (with wings open). Completed 1432. Oil and tempera on panel, 11' 3" × 14' 5". Sint Bavo, Ghent

VAN EYCK. The Ghent Altarpiece, upper half of left wing. 7′ × 3′ 6″. Adam stands in a niche beneath a lunette in grisaille showing Cain and Abel preparing the sacrifice. Singing angels gather around a lectern on which are carved two seated prophets and Saint Michael killing the dragon

ADAM

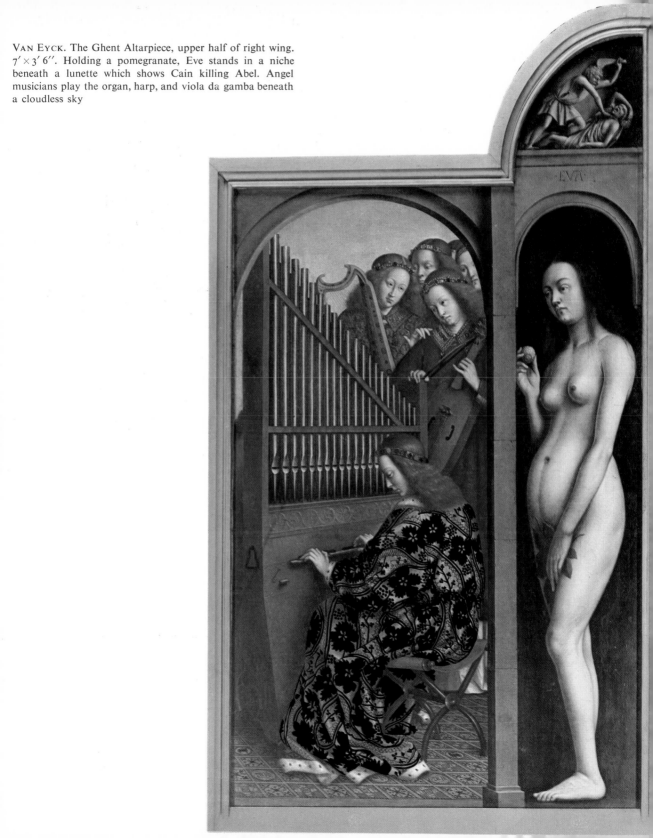

VAN EYCK. The Ghent Altarpiece, upper half of right wing.
7′ × 3′ 6″. Holding a pomegranate, Eve stands in a niche
beneath a lunette which shows Cain killing Abel. Angel
musicians play the organ, harp, and viola da gamba beneath
a cloudless sky

The technique of binding local colors into an over-all tone, precision in the rendering of the smallest and most subtle details such as plants and jewelry, intensification of the newly discovered world of things into something precious and, in consequence, sacred—all these were achievements of the Van Eyck brothers. They were made possible by new technical discoveries, and their influence was felt for centuries. After laying out the main features in drawing and shading as an underpainting, the final painting was done in resinous oil colors, that is, with tempera enriched by the addition of fatty, soft resinous substances. By this means, the undercoat of paint was not dissolved as previously, when the most that could be done in the way of overpainting was a few fine brush strokes applied with utmost prudence. Instead, it now became possible to work in broad surfaces and to deepen and saturate the color by successive glazes of paint laid on layer upon layer. Moreover, in the new technique, the brush stroke retained its original linear vitality, making possible a previously unknown precision in the rendering of the finest details such as hairs, leaves, or reflections of light on precious stones. The new realism was, nevertheless, balanced by a deep religiosity. If the Mother of God is made more immediately real to the suppliant, the eye is led into a remote far distance which makes of the sacred a world apart from the profane.

ROGIER VAN DER WEYDEN (1399?–1464). *Portrait of a Woman.* c. 1460. Oil and tempera on panel, 14¼ × 10½″. National Gallery, London ▶

Robert Campin, who is probably identical with the painter known as the Master of Flémalle, may have been a pupil of Jan van Eyck. He portrayed Saint Barbara in a room of his own time, and every detail of the Saint's person and setting is rendered with utmost realism. The attribute of her martyrdom—the tower in which she was imprisoned—is glimpsed through the window almost as if by accident. No halo sets the Saint apart from her environment. One might say that everything here has been made secular, but the artist views the newly discovered reality almost with awe, and all the allusions to sainthood are set down faithfully: the statue of the Throne of Mercy above the fireplace, the candles, the flowers of martyrdom, the ewer, the blazing fire. These things are depicted with such loving attention, as objects of beauty and value in themselves, that one overlooks the absence of a golden halo. Every object has its place, its function, its own physical existence as borne out by the shadow it casts, and yet all the objects are united in an order which transcends their simple, obvious meaning.

In such works as the Ghent Altarpiece and later in the *Madonna with Chancellor Rolin*, Van Eyck created the first portraits which were really true to nature. Thenceforth portrait painting would constitute a genre in itself. The details of physiognomy were observed in and for themselves, as unique traits to be found in no other person, and the artist employed his creative objectivity to unite the individual traits into a harmonious whole.

◀ ROBERT CAMPIN (1378?–1444), also known as the MASTER OF FLÉMALLE. *Saint Barbara.* 1438. Oil and tempera on panel, 39¾ × 18½″. The Prado, Madrid

ROGIER VAN DER WEYDEN. *Last Judgment*, central panel of an altarpiece. c. 1443–46. Oil and tempera on panel. Hôtel-Dieu, Beaune

The faithfulness to reality that the Van Eyck brothers strove for was a great step forward, a new and uncompromising advance. Those who followed them were left with the task of reconciling the innovation with
tradition. Thus, Rogier's portrait of a woman (page 175) is more abstract, more Gothic, than the face of
Van Eyck's Madonna (page 173). In Rogier's *Last Judgment*, for all that the individual details are true to
nature, once again they are subordinated to a rigid scheme of values. The artist's orderly spirit transformed
the new pictorial conceptions into forms which posterity was to exploit further.

Among those who followed Van Eyck, Hugo van der Goes was the greatest pioneer in overcoming the medieval tradition, above all in the effects of depth and physical space which he achieved. Figures and groups are no longer laid out parallel to the picture surface but emerge from the depths and intersect with other diagonals, and all of these lines lead to the Christ child as the central point of the composition as well as of the veneration of the various personages. The figures are given a convincing corporeal reality by color and contrasts in light. The scale of dimensions of the figures is further emphasized by gradations in color, so that the shepherds and the animals in the stalls are strikingly contrasted with the noble spirituality of the angels. Unreal and real are held in equilibrium, and a modern observation of nature combines with medieval conceptions of the reality of ideas to reveal to us how the Middle Ages understood the mystery of the Incarnation.

HUGO VAN DER GOES (1440–82). *Adoration of the Shepherds*, central panel of the Portinari Altarpiece. c. 1475–76. Oil and tempera on panel, 6′ 9″ × 9′ 10″. Uffizi Gallery, Florence

Konrad Witz (c. 1400–c. 1446). *Annunciation*. c. 1440–45. Oil and tempera on panel, $61^{1}/_{4} \times 47^{1}/_{4}''$. Germanisches Nationalmuseum, Nuremberg

The landscape stretching far into the depths of Bouts's *Saint Christopher* is as symbolic as that in Van Eyck's *Madonna with Chancellor Rolin* (page 173). It represents the Saint between the two banks of the river, at the moment of realization that it was the Creator of the World that he was carrying on his shoulders. The setting sun makes an aureole above the two figures. To heighten the miracle, the artist juxtaposed sharp contrasts within the narrowest of spaces. Thus, the remote distances fading into blueness are set against the red of the Saint's mantle which projects the image forward. The cramped, narrow space between the cliffs contrasts with the gigantic figure and with the broad expanse of water.

The most important successor to Van Eyck in the Germanic countries was Konrad Witz of Switzerland. One of the most consistent of the opponents of the "soft" International Gothic style, he championed the "hard" style which followed it in the regions north of the Alps. His settings are reduced to their bare essentials. The rafters casting a shadow on the Virgin, the plain handle on the door, the absence of any decorative furnishings, all serve to concentrate the eye on the two figures, which almost seem to burst out of the narrow space into which they are compressed. The light and shadow which fall on Mary are not mere notes of realism but, rather, symbols in accord with medieval conceptual thinking to which, despite all the artist's precise observation of reality, he remained bound.

◀ Dirck Bouts the Younger (c. 1448–90/91), attributed. *Saint Christopher Carrying the Christ Child*, right wing of an altarpiece called *The Pearl of Brabant*. Oil and tempera on oak panel, $24^{5}/_{8} \times 10^{7}/_{8}''$. Alte Pinakothek, Munich

LUKAS MOSER (active 1409–34). *Sea Voyage of Saint Mary Magdalen*, left wing of the Magdalen Altarpiece (slightly cut down in reproduction). 1431. Oil and tempera on panel, total dimensions $58^1/_2 \times 23^1/_4''$. Church of Sankt Maria Magdalena, Tiefenbronn (North Baden)

Konrad Witz went beyond the soft International style, but Lukas Moser, in his lyrical altarpiece which incorporates the discoveries of the Netherlanders, was still in the midst of the revolutionary change. Everything is idealized in the manner of Netherlandish and Burgundian miniatures: the broad expanse of the marine landscape, the background soaring up as a golden sky, the fine gradations in the crisp waves, the sailing vessels, and in the distance a city with a band of knights. A powerful shape filling the picture space, the rudderless ship floats on, driven by the currents to Marseilles where, legend says, the hostile pagans were first converted by these saints.

KONRAD WITZ. *The Miraculous Draught of Fishes.* 1444. Oil and tempera on panel, 52 × 60½″. Musée d'Art et d'Histoire, Geneva

Penetrating observation of nature led Konrad Witz to paint the first landscape which portrayed a real place, the shores of Lake Geneva. No longer does the artist compose with traditional pictorial formulas, but observes for himself the lay of the land. Yet, at the same time, he brings nature into relationship with the sacred event. The silhouette of the landscape seems to echo the grouping of the figures, and they acquire a new impressiveness through the timeless forms of nature.

The Master of the Annunciation of Aix reflects the influence of Netherlandish art in France. The setting of a church interior recalls the Washington *Annunciation* by Jan van Eyck in its adherence to the old notion that a church is an image of heaven. Even the differentiation in architecture is justified symbolically: the Angel is placed under a narrow baldachin decorated with statues of the prophets on the pillars and with winged creatures of the night in the spandrels, while behind Mary a broad Gothic interior opens out. Set against the uniform rhythm of the architecture, the figures stand out as an independent motif with their sumptuously colored garments, the full volumes of their bodies, and their firm relationship to each other.

MASTER OF THE ANNUNCIATION OF AIX. *Annunciation*, detail of an altarpiece. 1443/44. Oil and tempera on panel, complete dimensions 61 × 69¹/₄″. Sainte-Marie-Madeleine, Aix-en-Provence

The Women Drive the Prodigal Son out of Their House, detail of
a tapestry made for the Tuchers, a patrician family of Nuremberg. c. 1460. Germanisches Nationalmuseum, Nuremberg

Ever since the Apocalypse of Angers (page 158) and the Unicorn series (page 155), the tradition of tapestry
making flourished in the fifteenth century. It was considered best to remain within the limited pictorial
possibilities natural to the material and technique, avoiding the spatial elements and volumetric modeling
of the body which had become the rule in painted pictures. In fact, when the attempt was made in the sixteenth century to introduce those more modern traits, the results were not particularly happy. In the Late
Middle Ages, therefore, the colors were limited in range, though luminous, and the field of the picture was
filled uniformly.

HANS MULTSCHER (c. 1400–67). *The Road to Calvary*, from the Wurzach Altarpiece. 1437. Oil and tempera on panel, 58¼×55". State Museums, Berlin-Dahlem

Hans Multscher was one of the few artists of the Late Middle Ages with a double talent, equally powerful in expression as painter and sculptor. Under the influence of Burgundian and Netherlandish art, even in his early works he went beyond the flaccidity of the International Gothic style to attain a new expressive realism, as can be seen in his statue of the *Man of Sorrows* in the cathedral at Ulm. All lyricism was firmly ruled out. Instead, Multscher aimed to confront the believer entering the church with a starkly impressive image. In the Wurzach Altarpiece he went further even in rejecting idealization in favor of uncompromising realism. On a narrow stage tightly compressed by the framework, the events of the Passion take place with all the concentrated emotion of the moment. Bystanders with knife-sharp grimaces mock the Holy Women following the Cross and form a thick wall along their way. In the foreground, children throw stones at the condemned Christ who runs the gauntlet of the mob's fury, intimidated, bowed low under His burden. Yet here too the Man of Sorrows assumes impressive monumentality. The beam of the Cross separates Him from the grimacing crowd which brandishes weapons in the air menacingly. His face is presented frontally, fixing the viewer with His gaze, although the entire procession drives on energetically toward the right. Here too there is the motif of confrontation and challenge, instead of a religious image aiming only at beauty.

HANS MULTSCHER. *The Man of Sorrows.* c. 1429. Sandstone, height 66". West portal, Ulm Cathedral

JOHANN KOERBECKE (active 1446–91). *Calvary*, central panel of the Amelsbüren Altarpiece. Middle of fifteenth century. Oil and tempera on oak panel, 60×83″. Landesmuseum Münster (Westphalia)

Successive scenes are presented simultaneously here. At the left, Christ bearing the Cross passes through a city gate over whose portal is a heraldic animal holding a blank escutcheon. Behind the group is a couple with an infant. In the middle, centurions hold up vinegar to the crucified Christ and pierce His side. Below, in the foreground, John and the Holy Women support the fainting Mary, behind whom stands Mary Magdalen gazing up at the Cross. At the upper right is the Entombment, and below it Christ releases souls from Limbo while impotent devils vainly shoot at Him. Filling the entire picture surface densely with a simultaneous presentation of successive events was a peculiarity of North German and Westphalian art in particular. Such heavily populated scenes of Calvary were also frequent in carved wooden altarpieces. Memling's paintings of the Life of Mary provided a model for this type of picture, and many motifs in Koerbecke's *Calvary* suggest some connection with him and, especially, with the Master of Flémalle.

MASTER OF THE LIFE OF MARY (active c. 1470–80 in Cologne). *Madonna and Child on the Crescent Moon*. Oil and tempera on panel, 40¹/₂ × 30¹/₄″. Residenzmuseum, Bamberg

After the International Gothic period, representations of the Virgin changed greatly. The dominant note was no longer a childlike sweetness. Instead, she was shown as a forceful woman with a plain, homely, broad face, as in Multscher's paintings and statues. Once the realistic trend of the middle of the century had also done away with the treatment of drapery folds as an independent motif, in the 1460s the Madonna was given a new monumentality, and many realistic details were introduced into cycles on the Life of Mary. In the Dangolsheim Madonna one senses the hand of a powerful sculptor. He went back to the use of drapery folds for pictorial effect and as a means of heightening the force of an image, and in this he turned his back on the new realism and took up again the tradition of the "Beautiful Madonnas." The heavy, blocklike mass has virtually rectangular contours which, on the right, become almost a long, straight plumb line. This is peculiar to many statues of the time, and they are often designated as being in the "style of the long line." The sculptural mass is given spatial depth by deep hollows under the arms and by emphatic puffing out of the high-drawn mantle. In this work there seems to be a restless striving to go beyond realism in order to arrive at a new classicism.

Madonna and Child, from Dangolsheim, by a Strasbourg sculptor. c. 1470. Walnut with traces of old polychrome, height 40″. State Museums, Berlin-Dahlem. According to local tradition, the statue came from the Benedictine monastery at Schwarzach near Baden-Baden

MARTIN SCHONGAUER (c. 1430–91). *Adoration of the Shepherds.* c. 1475–80. Oil and tempera on oak panel 14³/₄ × 11″. State Museums, Berlin-Dahlem

The art of the Upper Rhine in the last quarter of the fifteenth century reveals the effort to incorporate realism into a new idealism, as we have seen in the Dangolsheim *Madonna.* The *Saint Catherine* from Obersimonswald, which is related to the workshop of the Dangolsheim master, recalls even more strongly the loveliness of the "Beautiful Madonnas." The sword with which the Saint was executed is almost hidden under her mantle, and even the bright red cloak, a symbol of her martyrdom, is used to create a lovely color harmony. The dramatic effect of the drapery folds is muted, and the mantle opens on a dress in a flowered pattern beneath which can be made out the forms of the body.

Closely related to the North German treatment of the face is the Mary in Schongauer's small picture, once the central panel of a house altar. Schongauer, who worked in Alsace, remained faithful to the training in drawing he received in his father's goldsmith's shop. Fine details are not brought out by color, as with Van Eyck, but by line. Schongauer must have conceived such pictures as engravings, without color, and then made a perfect transposition of color values into the expressive draftsmanship. This, however, testifies to his thoroughgoing feeling for color, as do also the gentle contrasts of blue, red, and green, as well as the juxtaposition of the luminous atmosphere of the background with the richer colors in the foreground. The excitement of the shepherds, the animal passivity of the ox and ass, and the various attributes symbolic of the Passion are all rendered in a muted key, and realism and piety are united here in a serene synthesis.

Saint Catherine. c. 1480. Painted wood, height c. 35¹/₂″. Obersimonswald, near Freiburg im Breisgau

Saint Christopher with the Christ Child. c. 1430. Woodcut, $11\frac{1}{8} \times 7\frac{7}{8}''$. By a southern German artist, probably from the Lake Constance region

PETER HEMMEL OF ANDLAU. *Madonna with Angels.* 1480–90. Detail of a stained-glass window, $17\frac{3}{4} \times 14\frac{5}{8}''$. Germanisches Nationalmuseum, Nuremberg

In the last years of the Middle Ages, Peter Hemmel of Andlau headed the most flourishing stained-glass workshop in southern Germany. From Alsace he exported works to Lorraine, Baden, Swabia, Hesse, Bavaria, and Austria, and his creations served as models for other workshops. They represent the last flowering of medieval glass painting (see also page 205). Characteristic are the relieflike, sharp delineation of the draped figures, the broad surfaces of the backgrounds with their glowing colored brocade patterns, and the way architectonic elements end up as naturalistic branches and leaves. Large panes and double panes were treated in painterly fashion, painted over with black lead which the artist then scraped away to create lines and highlights of the utmost delicacy.

In the fifteenth century the artistic mediums were enriched by new techniques which satisfied changing sociological needs. Woodcuts and copperplate engravings made devotional images available at modest prices to all strata of the population. Among the very earliest of these is this woodcut of Saint Christopher. There was a widespread popular belief that to look at his picture protected the believer from sudden death for that entire day, and this accounts for the wide diffusion of such images.

Woodcut from the *Biblia pauperum*, the so-called Bible of the Poor, which from 1430 on went through many editions as a woodcut book

The development of woodcuts and printed books went side by side. In the books, which were widely distributed after the middle of the fifteenth century, text and illustrations were cut into the same woodblock. At first, books were restricted to religious and didactic texts such as the *Ars moriendi* (The Art of Dying) and the *Bible of the Poor*. The latter was an expression of medieval typological thinking, in which scenes from the New Testament were juxtaposed to others from the Old Testament which were believed to prophesy, symbolically, the later events. In this woodcut from the *Biblia pauperum*, an architectural framework unites the various scenes: in the middle, the birth of Mary; at the left, the Tree of Jesse; at the right, Balaam's ass, which spoke and prophesied the sacred events; above and below, Old Testament prophets who foretold the Redemption.

After the woodcut, the copperplate engraving is the oldest graphic technique. Around 1440 it began to be used for the heraldic beasts on playing cards, but was soon adopted for devotional images intended for private use. The woodcut technique involves cutting away the wood from around the lines to be printed, so that they stand out in high relief. The copperplate technique, on the other hand, is related to goldsmith's work, in that extremely fine lines are incised into the plate and then filled in with ink and printed.

MASTER OF THE HOUSEBOOK. *The Children of Venus*. Pen drawing on paper, $9^1/_2 \times 5^3/_4$". Library, Wolfegg Castle (South Württemberg)

MASTER OF THE HOUSEBOOK. *Lovers.* Between 1480–90. Silverpoint on white-ground paper, $7^3/_4 \times 5^1/_4$". Kupferstich-kabinett, State Museums, Berlin-Dahlem

The Master of the Housebook was active between 1480 and 1490 in the Middle Rhine region, most likely in Mainz. Along with the Master of the Playing Cards, the Master E. S., and Martin Schongauer, he was one of the most influential copperplate engravers before Dürer. With dispassionate objectivity he observed the daily life of his time and set it down in his so-called Housebook in the form of sketches which have a remarkable precision of draftsmanship, comparable only to that employed in copperplate engraving. And yet, just as in the Book of Hours of the Limbourg brothers, however realistic the events he depicted might be, they are always set into their place in the vast cosmic order which governs the acts of men. Across the sky gallops the planet Venus, from the zodiac sign of Taurus, the Bull, to that of Libra, the Balance. Venus' children on earth, those born under her sign, give themselves without restraint to the pleasures of life, indulging in dancing, music, mixed bathing, and love-making. Thus, the Housebook, with its completely medieval presentation of events in simultaneity, is an invaluable source of information about the culture and customs of the time.

The morris dance came from Moorish Spain and quickly spread all over Europe in the Late Middle Ages as a form of social entertainment. It was a grotesque pantomime, ironic in character, and in it a dance-mad age mocked at itself. Sixteen of these statuettes, of which only ten survive, once danced on a turntable around a young maiden, ugly gnomes with foppish movements and lewd glances, to make up a picture of the foolishness of human behavior, another symbol of *Vanitas*. Such figures have the same meaning when found on the

ERASMUS GRASSER (c. 1450–1518). Morris Dancers, from the banqueting hall of the old town hall in Munich. c. 1480. Painted wood, heights ranging from $25^5/_8''$ to $31^1/_2''$. Stadtmuseum, Munich

large mechanical clocks in German towns, many of which still survive. Their bizarrely diversified, cross-legged, hectic movements, their weirdly demoniac expressions which ape strange psychological obsessions such as the dance epidemic which affected thousands in the Middle Ages, all make of these figures symptoms of their age and, at the same time, fine works of craftsmanship.

After the middle of the fifteenth century,
certain well-defined artistic personalities began to determine the course of sculpture as
well as painting, and there was an end to the
anonymity which, ever since the end of the
thirteenth century, had seemed to be the rule
in sculpture in the Northern countries, Peter
Parler excepted. The fact that the sculptors'
names are unknown to us, and the fact that it
is not even possible to attribute groups of
works to some anonymous but well-character-
ized personality, is typical of the position of
the sculptor in this period outside of Italy and
Spain. His art was at the service of the needs
of his time and completely bound up with
them, however timeless its message might be.
All that we can hope to do is to say when
and where certain works were done, using
as our basis specific traits in the general
conception, the body proportions, and, above
all, the special treatment of the drapery folds.
With the development of a humanistic con-
sciousness of the worth of the individual at the
end of the Late Middle Ages, a basic change
occurred. Even devotional images and the
great carved wooden altarpieces (in their way,
counterparts of the great programs of cathedral sculpture) came to be considered personal
tasks to be entrusted to responsible and
significant artists. Thus the personal, unmistakably typical conceptions of individual
sculptors came to predominate over the
generalized characteristics of the period,
though their works continued to obey these
and remained tied to the general development
of their time.

Death Disguised as a Monk. End of fifteenth century. Lime-wood, height 4¹/₈″. Badisches Landesmuseum, Karlsruhe. Facing page: detail of the skull

Realism here is carried so far that one can mistake this head under its monk's cowl for a real skull, and photographic enlargement makes the tiny statuette appear even more gruesome. It is scarcely likely that the figure was made as an isolated work. Probably it was part of a group of figures, perhaps a Dance of Death on a revolving disc or musical clock. One hand must have held an hourglass, the other a scythe. The image of death appeared over and over again as an impressive *Memento mori*.

Saint Christopher with the Christ Child, detail of the high altar in the parish church of Sankt Wolfgang, Kefermarkt, Austria, by a sculptor from Passau (MARTIN KRIECHBAUM? JÖRG HUBER?). c. 1490. Wood, formerly painted and gilded, approximately life-size

In the facial expression, with its intense gaze of remoteness from the world, the sculptor of the Saint Christopher on the facing page gives a spiritual significance to the Saint's task of carrying the Christ child.

CIRCLE OF PETER HEMMEL OF ANDLAU. *The Elector Philip I of the Palatinate*, from the parish church at Neckarsteinach near Heidelberg. 1483. Section of a stained-glass window, $36^5/_8 \times 21^5/_8''$. Hessisches Landesmuseum, Darmstadt. (See also page 192)

MASTER OF MOULINS (documented 1475–c. 1500). Triptych. 1499–1502. Oil and tempera on panel, 5′ 1³/₄″ × 9′ 3¹/₂″. Cathedral, Moulins. The Virgin in glory, surrounded by angels, is flanked by Pierre II, Duke of Bourbon, and Anne de Beaujeu

In France, the Master of Moulins, so named after his masterwork in the cathedral of that city, was the foremost artist in the transitional period between the Late Gothic and the Renaissance. He may, in fact, have been the painter Jean Perréal who was born in Paris in 1452, served the Bourbon family, and accompanied Charles VIII and Louis XII on their expeditions into Italy, where he met Leonardo da Vinci. Even more important than his contact with the Italian Renaissance was the influence of Flemish artists, especially Hugo van der Goes. Monumental treatment of the figure, bold coloring, and the contrast between large groups and an almost miniature-like atmosphere in the remote landscape all combine to achieve an impressive,

soaring solemnity. In contrast to the central panel, the side wings have an intimate character with their portraits of the donors, who are attended by their patron saints Peter and Anne. The donors' likenesses are still conceived with the objectivity of Netherlandish portraits, though they also reveal the master's striving after fidelity to nature. In their turn, these realistic portraits are contrasted with the angels which form a soaring halo around the Madonna (it is because of them that the artist is also designated as the Master of the Angels). The light radiating from the Madonna's aureole illuminates the faces of these angelic maidens of almost childlike grace, who are portrayed almost as if they were real persons.

Mary Magdalen (detail). c. 1500. Unpainted wood sculpture from Brabant. Cluny Museum, Paris

MICHAEL WOLGEMUT (1434–1519). Woodcuts from Hartmann Schädel, *Liber Chronicorum*, Nuremberg, 1493

Schädel's "World Chronicle," with something like two thousand illustrations, is the richest compendium of woodcuts of the fifteenth century. As both history and geography, its conception of the world as a global unity already reflects the new ideas of the Renaissance. Along with rather generalized portraits of great rulers, there are views of cities (like that of Basel below) which were the first attempts made to arrive at a precise and systematic topography. Nevertheless, occasionally the same view is used for several cities, and this is evidence that the old medieval typological approach had not been abandoned, as are also the woodcuts of the Dance of Death which appear in the course of and at the end of all the historical chapters.

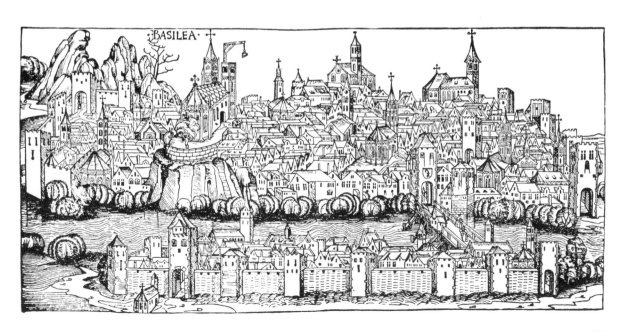

Royal Cloister, abbey of Santa Maria da ▶
Vitória, Batalha, Portugal. Second half of fifteenth century. The Manueline stonework
decoration seen here is attributed to Diogo
Boitac (d. c. 1522, leaving the work unfinished)

◀ South portal, east wing, abbey church of the
Convento do Cristo, Tomar, Portugal. The
east wing was added after 1510, and the south
portal, which is attributed to João do Castilho,
is dated 1515

The Late Gothic architecture of the end of the fifteenth century once again changed in character, not in general structural principles but, rather, in an organic proliferation of the individual architectonic elements. A high point of such exuberant architecture is found above all in Portugal, where the Islamic tradition heightened the Gothic style to the most elaborate sumptuosity, especially during the reign of Manoel I (1495–1521). The Manueline style is characterized by a Late Gothic flamboyance into which were introduced Renaissance elements.

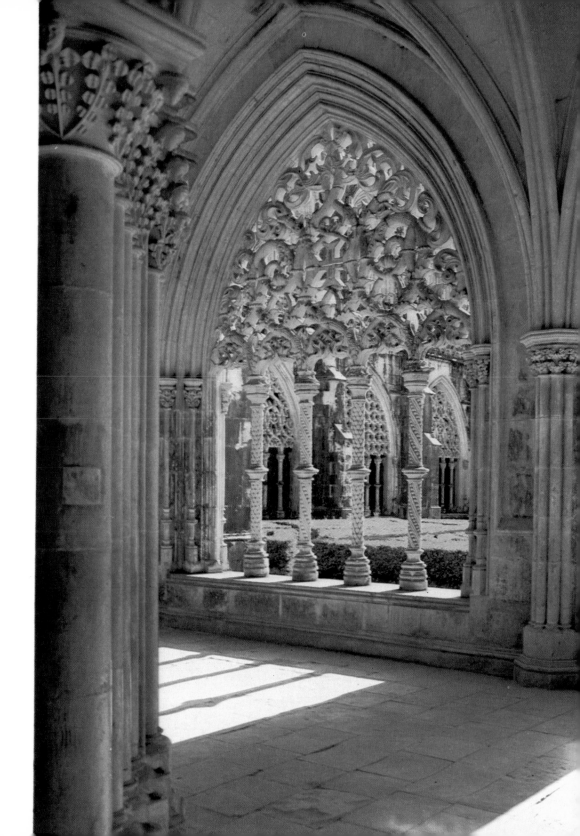

NIKLAUS VON HAGENAU (c. 1445–
1526). Presumed self-portrait.
c. 1495. Strasbourg Cathedral

Tomb effigy of Martín Vázquez de Arce. c. 1488.
Polychromed stone. Cathedral, Sigüenza, Spain

The personal portrait developed later in sculpture than in painting. In the mid-fifteenth century it began to develop out of the tradition of funeral monuments which showed the dead man as he had appeared in life. When painted portraits in the fifteenth century aimed at verisimilitude, it was with a neutral objectivity that transformed the sitter into something like a still life. Sculpture, however, with its corporeal energy which creates a sense of movement in space, was able also to capture the spiritual vitality of the subject. Remarkably early in date, on the tomb in Sigüenza the dead man is presented as in life, in an unaffected pose seemingly natural to his personality. In the self-portraits which architects left on the cathedrals, there is expressed even more of an individualistic creative energy. As Dürer was to demonstrate later in his portraits, some outward action or gesture, even if it were only an inclination of the head, heightens the expression of the subject's inner character.

HANS STETHAIMER (doc. 1441–59) (?). Portrait of the architect Hans von Burghausen. c. 1432. Stone, under life-size. Outer wall, south side of the church of Sankt Martin, Landshut. (See page 122)

◀ ANTON PILGRAM. (c. 1460–after 1515). Self-portrait looking through a window. 1515. Stone, under life-size. On the base of the pulpit, cathedral of Sankt Stephan, Vienna

HANS HOLBEIN THE ELDER (c. 1465–1524). *The Crowning with Thorns*, from the twelve-part "Gray Passion" cycle on the high altar of the Heiligkreuz Church, Augsburg. Shortly before 1499. Oil and tempera on panel, $35 \times 34^{1}/_{4}''$. Fürstlich Fürstenbergische Gemäldegalerie, Donaueschingen

◀ MICHAEL PACHER (c. 1435–98). *Coronation of the Virgin*, from a carved wooden altarpiece. 1471–75. Polychromed and gilded wood, figures about half life-size. Vintler Chapel, cemetery church, Gries, near Bolzano

TILMAN RIEMENSCHNEIDER (c. 1460–1531).
Eve (detail), from the chapel of the Virgin,
Würzburg. 1491–93. White sandstone, height
of entire figure 73″. Mainfränkisches Museum, Würzburg

TILMAN RIEMENSCHNEIDER. The Altarpiece
of the Holy Blood. 1501–5. Framework in pine,
figured panels in limewood, complete altarpiece with crowning figures and predella (not
shown) c. 26′ 3″ × 13′ 7″. Sankt Jacob, Rothenburg o. d. Tauber. Left: detail of a head
of an Apostle; pp. 222–23: the altarpiece with
the *Last Supper*, *Entry into Jerusalem*, and
Agony in the Garden. Above the shrine are
freestanding statues of angels holding a golden
Cross with the reliquary of the Holy Blood

The Würzburg sculptor and wood carver Tilman Riemenschneider achieved the first high point of his career
in the Altarpiece of the Holy Blood in Rothenburg. Earlier than other wood carvers, he replaced the traditional
polychrome and gilding of the figures with a sensitive treatment of the surface textures of the wood, and
exploited the natural grain of the wood as an expressive element in heads and hands. He took equal care with
the effect of carefully calculated lighting which falls on the group of Apostles, conferring his appropriate
character on each of them. In Riemenschneider's time it was still customary to line up individual figures in
a row, but he chose to group them in an interrelated dialogue, as the Naumburg Master had done much
earlier. Thus, the dialogue and action involve the entire table of the *Last Supper* and create a setting in depth
which is echoed by the concave space of the chapel-like structure of the scene; and that, in turn, is a kind of
miniature repetition of the glassed-in church choir in which the altarpiece stands.

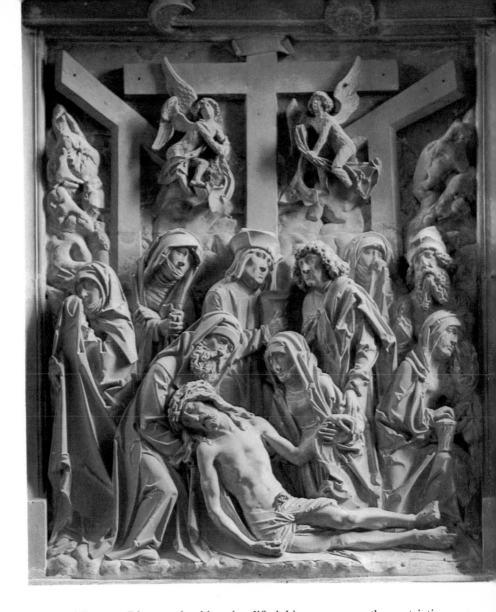

TILMAN RIEMENSCHNEIDER. *Head of the Doctor at the Sickbed of Emperor Henry II*, detail of the relief of *Saint Benedict Curing the Emperor of the Stone* on the tomb of Henry II. 1499–1513. Solnhofen limestone, considerably smaller than the photograph. Bamberg Cathedral

TILMAN RIEMENSCHNEIDER. *Lamentation over the Dead Christ*, altarpiece. 1519–23. Gray sandstone, $98^1/_2 \times 65^1/_2''$. Former Cistercian church, Maidbronn

In his last work, the altarpiece at Maidbronn, Riemenschneider simplified his means greatly, restricting himself to what was most essential. Without action, dialogues, or secondary groupings to distract the eye of the viewer from the central event, the altarpiece is entirely concentrated on a single point in the center below the stone shrine, and only by directing the gaze to that point do the foreshortenings and perspective relationships of the three crosses become intelligible. As the figures emerge from the shallow relief of the background, they become increasingly three-dimensional until, in the immediate foreground, they culminate in the Christ, the only figure which is entirely sculpted in the round. Empty intervals of silent space separate the heads one from the other. Each head is related to its neighbors only by the common bond of an expression of personal grief. Even Mary's gaze is directed beyond her dead Son. At either side of the group, in an extraordinary stroke of imagination, a woman turns away to hide her weeping. What Riemenschneider left us here, at the end of his creative life, was a mournful lamentation impregnated with resignation.

Though the art of Veit Stoss had its roots in Nuremberg, he assimilated all the great achievements of German sculpture before him, from Nicolaus Gerhaerts to the Dangolsheim Madonna. His creative genius was of the kind one would expect of a Renaissance artist, but he also represents the final perfection of Gothic art. In 1477 he renounced his citizenship of Nuremberg to settle in Cracow. There, for the German community, he carved the most imposing wooden altar of late-medieval art, a structure more than forty-two feet high and thirty-six feet wide. The heads of the Apostles have thoroughly human traits, differentiated in character and full of individual personality. He returned to Nuremberg in 1496, and his last altarpiece was carved for Bamberg. The pathos of his work in Cracow was muted in the Bamberg altar, and the composition is rigorously unified for all its diversity. With deeply expressive emphasis he introduced premonitions of the Passion into the Christmas scene: alongside the Infant—a tiny and inconspicuous figure in the over-all composition—there are seen the cave where Christ was entombed, the tall column of His flagellation, and in the background the soldiers of Pontius Pilate, who look on, peacefully, at the miracle of the Nativity.

TILMAN RIEMENSCHNEIDER. *Hands of the Dead Christ, Mary, and Saint John,* detail of the Maidbronn altarpiece (see page 225)

VEIT STOSS. *Hands of the Virgin,* ▶ detail of the Altarpiece of the Virgin in Cracow (see page 226)

With Veit Stoss, as with Riemenschneider, hands were a major element of expression. The soft limewood which he used permitted modeling of the utmost sensitivity in the rendering of veins and tendons. In their carving of hands, both masters achieved something beyond complete fidelity to nature. They visualized the hand in relation to the entire figure, as a reflection of the total expressive content, whether it be relaxed trust or nervous determination.

Hieronymus Bosch is one of the most fascinating exponents of the radical change from the Middle Ages to modern times. Little that came before him seems to point the way to his innovations. His roots lie in Netherlandish painting, from whose spirituality (which was more and more oriented toward real things) he turned away. His predecessors and contemporaries were increasingly concerned with a more precise rendering of real things in space and atmosphere, but he took an opposite path and rejected what his age had learned from observing natural phenomena. What he sought was an expression of spiritual reality. He was concerned on the one hand with ideas of temptation and sin, on the other with merciful redemption. With such a profoundly medieval conception, which scorned the humanistic ideas concerning the value of the individual, the demons and chimeras of the cathedrals returned to art. And yet Bosch reached far beyond his own time, beyond its notions of human self-awareness. He explored the deeper regions of men's minds, penetrating to realms which would remain uncomprehended until the advent of psychoanalysis. To man's inner essence he applied criteria which belong to the deepest bases of human existence.

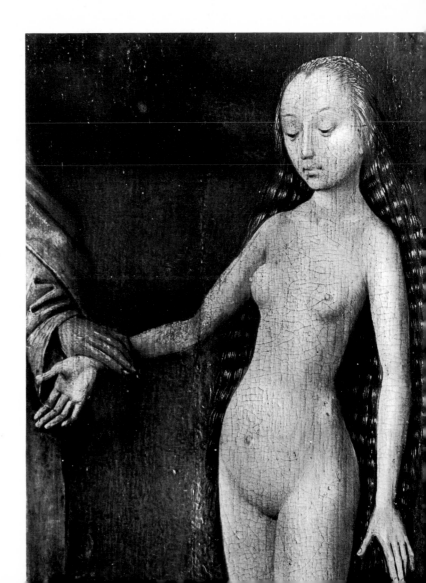

HIERONYMUS BOSCH (c. 1450–1516). *The Garden of Delights*, triptych. 1503–4. Central panel $86^1/_2 \times 76^3/_4''$, wings $86^1/_2 \times 38''$ each. The Prado, Madrid. Facing page: *Paradise* (detail of left wing). Right: *Eve Brought to Adam by God* (detail of left wing). Overleaf: *Hell* (detail of right wing). Page 233: *Lovers in a House Made of the Pomegranate of Temptation* (detail of central panel)

MATTHIAS GRÜNEWALD (c. 1470–1528). The Isenheim Altarpiece, view with wings closed. Completed 1515. Oil and tempera on panel; central panel 8′ 10″ (maximum height) ×10′ 1″; lateral stationary panels 7′ 7$\frac{1}{2}$″ ×c. 2′ 6″ each; predella 26$\frac{3}{8}$″ ×11′ 2$\frac{1}{4}$″ (maximum width). Musée d'Unterlinden, Colmar

With the wings closed we see: the central panel with the crucified Christ, and at the left Mary, John, and Mary Magdalen, at the right the sacrificial lamb with chalice and crosier and John the Baptist, above whose right arm is the inscription *Illum oportet crescere me autem minui* (He must grow, and

I diminish); the predella with the Entombment attended by Mary, John, and Mary Magdalen; the right panel with Saint Anthony the Hermit attired as a prebendary in the Anthonin order of Isenheim; the left panel with Saint Sebastian and angels descending from Heaven to bring him the martyr's crown.

MATTHIAS GRÜNEWALD. The Isenheim Altarpiece, second view with wings opened: central panel with the *Nativity*, 8′ 8″ (maximum height) × 10′. The left wing (not reproduced here) has the *Annunciation*, the right wing the *Resurrection* (see page 238)

The central panel, in this view, has at the left a Gothic baldachin, beneath which angels join in a concert of celebration of the birth of Christ. To the right of the baldachin there is a female figure with a luminous aureole who turns in adoration toward the right half of the picture. She may be meant to represent Eve as the precursor of Mary. At the right, Mary sits on a stone bench in an open landscape, although the household objects associated with the lying-in room appear around her. She holds the Infant on a cloth which is in shreds, recalling that seen in the Entombment on the predella. To the left above her, the sky opens to reveal God the Father in a a gloriole of golden rays, dispatching myriads of angel-like creatures of light to join in the adoration. In the mountains,

236

an angel bears the good tidings to the shepherds. Throughout the picture there are symbolic allusions to the Lorettine Litany to the Madonna: the closed garden, the rose without thorns, the house of God, and the like.

Opened fully, for the third view, the altarpiece reveals, in the center, a statue group carved by Niklaus von Hagenau: Saint Anthony enthroned, flanked by Saints Augustine and Jerome. Opened, the predella has carved statuettes of Christ and the twelve Apostles by the same sculptor. The side wings, painted by Grünewald, have at the left the hermit-saints Anthony and Paul (detail on page 239), and at the right the *Temptation of Saint Anthony*, which includes demoniac motifs recalling those in the paintings of Bosch and Schongauer.

MATTHIAS GRÜNEWALD. The Isenheim Altarpiece, right wing of the second view, flanking the *Nativity*: the *Resurrection*, in which Christ's body appears transfigured. 8′ 10″ (maximum height, not fully shown here) × 4′ 8¼″

MATTHIAS GRÜNEWALD. The Isenheim Altarpiece, left wing of the third view, flanking the statues: *The Meeting of the Hermits Anthony and Paul in the Desert* (detail). Tradition has it that the head of Paul, seen here, is a self-portrait of the artist.

Mathis Gothart Nithart was the real name of the painter who, because of the biographer Sandrart's error, has entered art history as Matthias Grünewald. His masterpiece was painted for the high altar of the church in the Anthonin order's hospital at Isenheim. It is an immense synthesis of medieval symbolism, modern observation of nature, and the expressive power in figurative and coloristic composition which is entirely unique to this painter. His work is in complete opposition to the formal concepts of the Italian Renaissance (which had an incomparably greater influence on his contemporary Dürer). He made a radical break with the logic of figural proportions, conceiving them entirely on the basis of symbolic associations. Interiors and landscapes interpenetrate in a wholly unrealistic manner, as in the household objects seen in the *Nativity*. Light is used not as a means of illumination but as a mystical revelation. Inspired by the visions of Saint Bridget of Sweden, Grünewald even made modifications in the textual traditions of the Scriptures: at the scene of the Crucifixion he introduced the long-dead John the Baptist, who had never been associated with that event; with the Resurrection, he combined the idea of the Transfiguration and Ascension in the slow transformation of the human body of Christ as it becomes impregnated with the divine light. As a direct parallel to humanistic rationalism, and in part with means borrowed from it, the artist set down in paint the reality of an inconceivable mystery.

In the same way as in the painting of Grünewald and that of the Master of Messkirch who was inspired by him (see page 242), in the sculpture of the beginning of the sixteenth century there also arises the question of the particular character of the German Renaissance. The sculpture of the so-called Master H. L., whose workshop in Breisach was responsible for the altarpiece in nearby Niederrottweil, pictured here, as well as the early-sixteenth-century works shown in the following pages, are evidence that, concurrently with the influence of the Italian Renaissance, many German centers and their artists clung to Gothic traditions. To the more intellectual humanism of their time, they opposed the passionately heightened pathos of the older art. In this period of crisis around 1500, German art found its separate way. It returned to the intricate linearity of the Germanic ornamental style with its highly complex interlacing patterns; and these seem also to anticipate the Romantic attitude, with their melancholy feeling for nature and their enigmatic mystique of light.

WORKSHOP OF MASTER H. L. *Christ Saviour of the World*, detail of the predella of the altarpiece on the facing page

WORKSHOP OF MASTER H. L. Altarpiece on the high altar, Sankt Michael, Niederrottweil (Breisgau). 1525–30. Polychromed carved wood. The subjects on the wings are related in crisscross fashion: on the upper left is Saint Michael weighing souls on Judgment Day, and on the lower right is the repudiation of the damned souls; on the lower left is John the Baptist baptizing Christ, and on the upper right the beheading of John at the instigation of Salome. In the predella are Christ and the Apostles (detail on facing page)

MASTER OF MESSKIRCH (active c. 1500–c. 1545). *Saint Christopher and the Christ Child*, from the left-hand panel of the Falkenstein Altarpiece. c. 1530–40. Oil and tempera on canvas over spruce-wood, $20\frac{1}{8} \times 12\frac{1}{4}''$. Fürstlich Fürstenbergische Gemäldegalerie, Donaueschingen

The wood carver Heinrich Douvermann created one of the masterworks of Late Gothic of the Lower Rhine in his Altarpiece of the Virgin in Xanten. Swirling rootlike scrolls grow from the breast of the sleeping Jesse, and in their coils can be made out the genealogy of Mary. In form, they recall ancient Germanic and Celtic ornamental motifs. The organic character of the so-called "Gothic root style," whose decorative motifs appeared on tombstones and the portals of small churches at the start of the sixteenth century, was exploited here in a conception born out of the very subject itself, to create something replete with spiritual significance.

HEINRICH DOUVERMANN. *The Sleeping Jesse*, from the predella pictured below

HEINRICH DOUVERMANN (active 1510–44). Predella with the Tree of Jesse, in the Altarpiece of the Virgin. Completed 1535. Wood, height c. 31½″. Cathedral of Sankt Viktor, Xanten

◀ HEINRICH DOUVERMANN. *Angels with Censers*,
on the Altarpiece of the Virgin, cathedral of
Sankt Viktor, Xanten
▼

HANS BRÜGGEMANN (c. 1480–1540). *Lute-Playing Angel*, probably from the tabernacle in the Marienkirche, Husum. 1520. Oak, height 15³/₄″. State Museums, Berlin-Dahlem

BERNT NOTKE (c. 1435/40–1509). ▶ *Saint George and the Dragon with the Princess of Libya.* Completed 1489. Polychromed wood, 9′ 10″ × 7′ 6″. Church of Sankt Nikolai, Stockholm

In the group of Saint George and the Dragon (facing page) the princess whom legend says the Saint rescued looks across at the combat. This monumental work was commissioned from the Lübeck sculptor by the Swedish Imperial Administrator Sten Sture as a national victory memorial.

WORKSHOP OF HANS LEINBERGER (c. 1480
-1531/35). *The Martyrdom of Saint
Castulus.* c. 1513. Wood relief, $46^1/_2 \times 41^3/_4''$.
Collegiate church, Moosburg

Hans Leinberger was active in Landshut in Bavaria from 1513 to 1530. Together with Grünewald and the Master H. L., he belongs among the exponents of a typically South German, dynamically expressive Late Gothic style. Yet he is less of a symbolist than a dramatically impassioned narrator. This is seen in his striking use of architectonic and landscape elements and also in the rigor of his compositions, from which all embellishments are banned. These are traits which also relate him to the so-called Danube School of painting. Characteristic of his sculpture are the deep, convoluted, basinlike swirls of the drapery which conceal the body, and the surfaces and contours of his figures are crinkled in a way that makes it seem as if the form itself were about to decompose.

HANS LEINBERGER. *Madonna*, presumed to come from the town hall of Moosburg. c. 1519. Bronze, height 18¹/₈″. State Museums, Berlin-Dahlem

The transition from Late Gothic to Renaissance was much more marked in France than in Germany because of the influence of Italian Renaissance art, whose way had been prepared long before, in Avignon, by the introduction of the Southern feeling for form. At Chartres, within the Gothic architectural framework of the choir screen are set scenes in which the spatial unity is clearly articulated and the individual forms have a classical perfection. At Brou there is something similar. There, almost nothing apart from the style of the drapery folds remains to recall the Gothic tradition. All individual forms, and their rigorous alignment according to horizontal and vertical principles, are conceived in the spirit of the Renaissance.

Choir screen, Chartres Cathedral. Beginning of sixteenth century. Stone. Left: part of the screen with scenes from the life of Mary set into the architectural framework as if on small stages. Above: head of the Virgin from the Adoration of the Magi on the choir screen

The Virgin, detail of the *Annunciation* in the Altarpiece of the ▶ Seven Joys of Mary, by a Franco-Flemish sculptor. 1528. Choir of the abbey church of Saint-Nicolas, Brou (Eure-et-Loir)

In Germany, the centers which had closer contact with the art of the Italian Renaissance were the commercial cities of the south, above all Augsburg, Nuremberg, and Basel. But even in works in which Italian influence is obvious, it made difficult headway against the Late Gothic feeling for form. Such influence was, in fact, much more closely linked to a typical native exuberant formal fantasy, and that was hard to reconcile with the Italian clarity and firm delineation of form. The allegorical figures of Peter Dell are excellent illustrations of the conflict which resulted. Their familiarity with the human body, the functional co-ordination of the limbs in a dance movement, the realization of equilibrium through countermovements, the marked worldliness of the conception—all of these would have been unthinkable without influence from the aristocratic Italian Renaissance. Nevertheless, the handling of the garments swirling around the body, with their folds which unexpectedly take on a life of their own, the naked leg emerging almost surreptitiously from the dark hollow of the garment, the contrast between the organic form of the body and the billowing wave of the drapery—these belong to a native tradition, a mannerism which grew out of the Late Gothic, and Mannerism was a style to which the art of the countries north of the Alps were destined to make a significant contribution in the sixteenth century.

PETER DELL THE ELDER. *Allegory of Lust*, from a series of the Seven Deadly Sins. c. 1530. Wood, height 10³/₄″. Germanisches Nationalmuseum, Nuremberg

Bibliography

GENERAL LITERATURE

AUBERT, M., *Art of the High Gothic Era*, New York, 1964
BRIEGER, P., *English Art, 1216–1307*, New York, 1957
DEHIO, G., *Geschichte der deutschen Kunst*, Berlin, 1923, Vol. 2
EVANS, J., *Art in Mediaeval France, 987–1498*, New York, 1948
EVANS, J., *English Art, 1307–1461*, New York, 1949
EVANS, J., ed., *The Flowering of the Middle Ages*, London and New York, 1966
FRANKL, P., *The Gothic: Literary Sources and Interpretations through Eight Centuries*, Princeton, 1960
HUIZINGA, J., *The Waning of the Middle Ages*, New York, 1954
JANTZEN, H., *High Gothic*, New York, 1962
LEFRANÇOIS-PILLION, L., *L'Art du quatorzième siècle en France*, Paris, 1954
MÂLE, E., *L'Art allemand et l'art français du moyen-âge*, Paris, 1940
MÂLE, E., *L'Art religieux de la fin du moyen-âge en France*, Paris, 1949
TOESCA, P., *Il Trecento*, Turin, 1951
WEISE, G., *Italien und die geistige Welt der Gotik*, Halle an der Saale, 1939
WHITE, J., *Art and Architecture in Italy: 1250–1400*, Baltimore, 1966
WORRINGER, W., *Form in Gothic*, New York, 1964

ARCHITECTURE

AUBERT, M., *Gothic Cathedrals of France*, London, 1959
BAUM, J., ed., *German Cathedrals*, New York, 1956
BOOZ, P., *Der Baumeister der Gotik*, Munich and Berlin, 1956
BRANNER, R., *Burgundian Gothic Architecture*, London, 1960
BRANNER, R., *St. Louis and the Court Style in Gothic Architecture*, London, 1965
CLASEN, K. H., *Deutsche Gewölbe der Spätgotik*, Berlin, 1958
FITCHEN, J., *The Construction of Gothic Cathedrals*, New York, 1961
FRANKL, P., *Gothic Architecture*, Baltimore, 1962
KNOOP, D., and JONES, G. P., *The Medieval Mason*, Manchester, 1933
PANOFSKY, E., *Abbot Suger on the Abbey Church of St. Denis and its Art Treasures*, Princeton, 1946
PANOFSKY, E., *Gothic Architecture and Scholasticism*, New York, 1957
SEDLMAYR, H., *Die Entstehung der Kathedrale*, Zurich, 1950
SIMSON, O. VON, *The Gothic Cathedral*, New York, 1956
TORRES BALBÁS, L., *Arquitectura gótica* (Ars Hispaniae VII), Madrid, 1952
WEBB, G., *Architecture in Britain: The Middle Ages*, Baltimore, 1956

SCULPTURE

AUBERT, M., *La Sculpture française au moyen-âge*, Paris, 1947
DURÁN SANPERE, A., and AINAUD DE LASARTE, J., *Escultura gótica* (Ars Hispaniae VII!), Madrid, 1956
JANTZEN, H., *Deutsche Bildhauer des 13. Jahrhunderts*, Leipzig, 1925
JANTZEN, H., *Über den gotischen Kirchenraum und andere Aufsätze*, Berlin, 1951
KATZENELLENBOGEN, A., *The Sculptural Programs of Chartres Cathedral*, Baltimore, 1959
MÜLLER, T., *Sculpture in the Netherlands, Germany, France, and Spain: 1400–1500*, Baltimore, 1966
PINDER, W., *Die deutsche Plastik des 14. Jahrhunderts*, Munich, 1925
POPE-HENNESSY, J., *Italian Gothic Sculpture*, Greenwich, Conn., 1955
STONE, L., *Sculpture in Britain: The Middle Ages*, Baltimore, 1955
VITRY, P., *French Sculpture during the Reign of St. Louis: 1226–1270*, Florence and New York, 1929

PAINTING

AUBERT, M., and others, *Le Vitrail français*, Paris, 1958
BAKER, J., *English Stained Glass*, New York, 1960
COLETTI, L., *I Primitivi*, Novara, 1941–47, 3 vols.
MARCHINI, G., *Italian Stained Glass Windows*, New York, 1956
MARLE, R. VAN, *The Development of the Italian Schools of Painting*, The Hague, 1923–38
MATĚJČEK, A., and PEŠINA, J., *Czech Gothic Painting*, Prague, 1953
PANOFSKY, E., *Early Netherlandish Painting*, Cambridge, Mass., 1953, 2 vols.
PORCHER, J., *Medieval French Miniatures*, New York, 1959
POST, C. R., *A History of Spanish Painting*, Cambridge, Mass., 1930–41, Vols. 2–8
RICKERT, M., *Painting in Britain: The Middle Ages*, Baltimore, 1954
RING, G., *A Century of French Painting, 1400–1500*, Greenwich, Conn., 1949
STANGE, A., *Deutsche Malerei der Gotik*, Berlin, 1938–60, Vols. 3–10
THOMPSON, D. V., *The Materials and Techniques of Medieval Painting*, New York, 1957
TINTORI, L., and MEISS, M., *Painting of the Life of St. Francis in Assisi*, New York, 1962
TOESCA, P., *Florentine Painting of the Trecento*, Florence, 1929
WEIGELT, C., *Sienese Painting of the Trecento*, New York, 1936
WENTZEL, H., *Meisterwerke der Glasmalerei*, Berlin, 1951

European Painting from 1350 to 1520

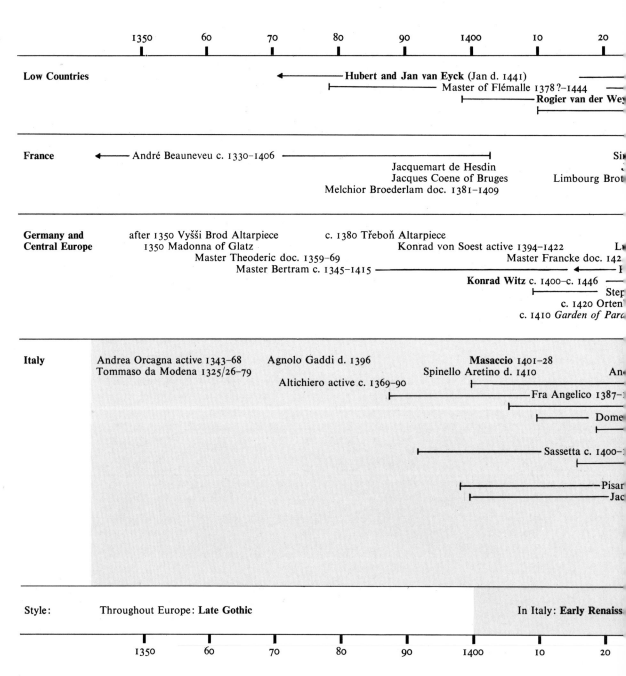

Low Countries

← — Hubert and Jan van Eyck (Jan d. 1441) ————
├——————— Master of Flémalle 1378?–1444
├——————— Rogier van der Wey

France

← — André Beauneveu c. 1330–1406 ———————— Si

Jacquemart de Hesdin
Jacques Coene of Bruges   Limbourg Brot
Melchior Broederlam doc. 1381–1409

Germany and Central Europe

after 1350 Vyšši Brod Altarpiece   c. 1380 Třeboň Altarpiece
1350 Madonna of Glatz   Konrad von Soest active 1394–1422   L
Master Theoderic doc. 1359–69   Master Francke doc. 142
Master Bertram c. 1345–1415 ————————← — F
Konrad Witz c. 1400–c. 1446 ——— Ste
├—— Step
c. 1420 Orten
c. 1410 *Garden of Para*

Italy

Andrea Orcagna active 1343–68   Agnolo Gaddi d. 1396   **Masaccio** 1401–28
Tommaso da Modena 1325/26–79   Spinello Aretino d. 1410   An
Altichiero active c. 1369–90
├——————— Fra Angelico 1387–
├——————— Dome
├——————— Sassetta c. 1400–
├——————— Pisar
├——————— Jac

Style:

Throughout Europe: **Late Gothic**   In Italy: **Early Renaiss**

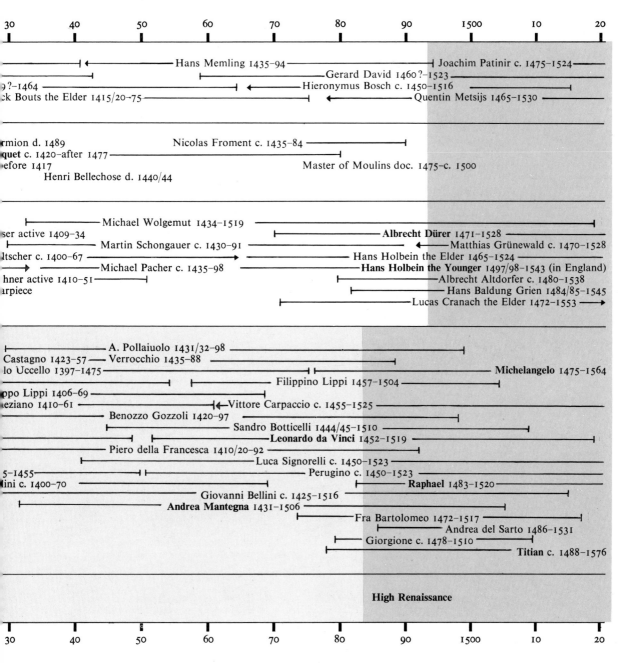

30   40   50   60   70   80   90   1500   10   20

─────── ←──────── Hans Memling 1435–94 ─────── Joachim Patinir c. 1475–1524 ──────
9?–1464 ──────── ├──────── Gerard David 1460?–1523 ──────────
:k Bouts the Elder 1415/20–75 ──────── ├── ←────── Hieronymus Bosch c. 1450–1516 ──────
                                          ←────── Quentin Metsijs 1465–1530 ──────

rmion d. 1489   Nicolas Froment c. 1435–84 ───────
quet c. 1420–after 1477 ──────
efore 1417   Master of Moulins doc. 1475–c. 1500
    Henri Bellechose d. 1440/44

├──────── Michael Wolgemut 1434–1519 ────────
ser active 1409–34   ├──────── **Albrecht Dürer** 1471–1528 ────────
├──────── Martin Schongauer c. 1430–91 ──────── ←──── Matthias Grünewald c. 1470–1528
ltscher c. 1400–67 ──────────────────→ ──────── Hans Holbein the Elder 1465–1524 ──────
──→ ├──── Michael Pacher c. 1435–98 ──────── **Hans Holbein the Younger** 1497/98–1543 (in England)
hner active 1410–51 ──────── ──────── Albrecht Altdorfer c. 1480–1538
arpiece   ├──────── Hans Baldung Grien 1484/85–1545
                              ├──────── Lucas Cranach the Elder 1472–1553 ──→

├──────── A. Pollaiuolo 1431/32–98 ──────────
Castagno 1423–57 ── Verrocchio 1435–88 ──────────
lo Uccello 1397–1475 ──────── **Michelangelo** 1475–1564
ppo Lippi 1406–69 ──────── ├──── Filippino Lippi 1457–1504 ────────
eziano 1410–61 ── ←── Vittore Carpaccio c. 1455–1525 ──────
├──── Benozzo Gozzoli 1420–97 ──────── Sandro Botticelli 1444/45–1510 ────────
Piero della Francesca 1410/20–92 ──────── **Leonardo da Vinci** 1452–1519 ────────
├──── Luca Signorelli c. 1450–1523 ────────
5–1455 ──────── ├── Perugino c. 1450–1523 ────────
lini c. 1400–70 ──────── **Raphael** 1483–1520 ────────
    Giovanni Bellini c. 1425–1516 ────────
    Andrea Mantegna 1431–1506 ────────
                    Fra Bartolomeo 1472–1517 ────────
                        Andrea del Sarto 1486–1531
                    ├──── Giorgione c. 1478–1510 ────
                                Titian c. 1488–1576

High Renaissance

30   40   50   60   70   80   90   1500   10   20

255

Sculpture and Painting

		France	Germany and Central Europe
13th C.	Sculpture	Cathedral Sculpture: Chartres, north and south porches, c. 1217 Paris: Portal of the Virgin, 1210–20; Last Judgment Portal (in original form), 1225–30; *Porte Rouge*, 1270 Reims: north portal, c. 1220–30; west portal, c. 1236–52; Master of St. Joseph, c. 1240; west inner wall, c. 1255 on Amiens: west portal, c. 1230; *Vierge dorée*, c. 1270	1220 on, Strasbourg, south portal and statue of Angel on pilaster 1230, Wechselburg, Crucifixion group on chancel arch c. 1230–37, Bamberg, choir screen, *Fürstenportal*, statue of King on Horseback 1250–70, Naumburg Master active in Naumburg c. 1280 on, Strasbourg, west portal 1285–1300, Master of the Erminold Tomb active in Regensburg c. 1280–1310, Freiburg, statues in the porch
	Painting	1223–30, Psalter of St. Louis and Blanche of Castile 1253–70, Psalter of St. Louis c. 1260, Gospel Lectionary of the Sainte-Chapelle c. 1295, Breviary of Philip the Fair	c. 1225, frescoes in Soest before 1250, Soest, altarpiece 1240–60, Gurk, frescoes in gallery c. 1250, Quedlinburg, altarpiece 1230–70, Cologne, Sankt Maria Lyskirchen, frescoes
14th C.	Sculpture	1339, Silver Madonna of Jeanne d'Évreux Paris School, ivory carvings c. 1370, statues of Charles V and Jeanne de Bourbon from the Celestine abbey, Paris 1385–1406, Claus Sluter in Dijon 1384–1410, tomb of Philip the Bold	Devotional images, Christ with St. John statues Vesper images, realistic crucifixes c. 1350, Bamberg, tomb of Friedrich von Hohenlohe 1375–93, Prague, busts in triforium 1385–96, Nuremberg, *Schöner Brunnen* (fountain) c. 1400, Český Krumlov, "Beautiful Madonnas"
	Painting	1316–17, *Vie de Saint-Denis* 1323–26, Breviary of Belleville, by Jean Pucelle 1325–28, *Livre d'Heures de Jeanne d'Évreux* c. 1330–1406, André Beauneveu doc. 1381–1409, Melchior Broederlam	1300 on, Cologne School of painting c. 1320, Manesse Codex 1350, Madonna of Glatz after 1350, Master of Vyšši Brod active 1359–69, Master Theoderic 1380 on, Master of Třeboň c. 1345–1415, Bertram of Minden
15th–16th C. For painting, see the chronological chart, European Painting from 1350 to 1520	Sculpture	c. 1370–1439, Claus de Werve c. 1425–c. 1494, Antoine le Moiturier c. 1430–1512, Michel Colombe	c. 1400–67, Hans Multscher d. 1473, Nicolaus Gerhaerts of Leiden c. 1425–93, Jörg Syrlin the Elder c. 1435–98, Michael Pacher c. 1435/40–1509, Bernt Notke c. 1450–1518, Erasmus Grasser c. 1445–1526, Niklaus von Hagenau c. 1445–1533, Veit Stoss c. 1455/60–1508/9, Adam Krafft c. 1460–after 1515, Anton Pilgram c. 1460–1531, Tilman Riemenschneider active 1513–30, Hans Leinberger active 1523–30, Master H. L. c. 1480–1540, Hans Brüggemann

England	Italy
c. 1200–10, Wells, tomb of Bishop Levericus 1225–30, Worcester, tomb of King John 1230–40, Salisbury, tomb of William Longespée 1260–65, Lincoln, *Ecclesia* and *Synagogue* 1282–84, Hereford, tomb of Thomas de Cantelupe 1291–93, London, Westminster Abbey, tomb of Queen Eleanor of Castile	c. 1225, Lucca, statue of St. Martin c. 1225–c. 1287, Nicola Pisano c. 1240–1302, Arnolfo di Cambio c. 1248–after 1314, Giovanni Pisano
1250, Apocalypse of St. Albans 1250, Psalter of Salisbury c. 1240–60, Missal of Henry of Chichester 1250–59, *Historia Anglorum*, by Matthew Paris	Berlinghiero Berlinghieri active c. 1235–c. 1250, Giunta Pisano 1266/67–1337, Giotto 1272, Cimabue in Rome 1278–1319, Duccio in Siena
Nottingham, alabaster reliefs 1330–35, Gloucester, tomb of Edward II 1340, London, Westminster Abbey, tomb of John of Eltham 1348–50, Oxford, tomb of Elizabeth Montagu 1350–65, Exeter, royal statues on west front 1377–80, Canterbury, tomb of the Black Prince	c. 1275–1330, Lorenzo Maitani c. 1285–1337, Tino da Camaino c. 1270–before 1358, Andrea Pisano active 1343–68, Andrea Orcagna 1364–1438, Jacopo della Quercia
1330, Psalter of Saint-Omer 1330–55, Psalter of Robert de Lisle	1284–1344, Simone Martini 1300–34, Pietro Cavallini active 1317–47, Lippo Memmi 1306–48, Pietro Lorenzetti d. c. 1348, Bernardo Daddi doc. 1319–c. 1348, Ambrogio Lorenzetti active 1332–66, Taddeo Gaddi 1325/26–79, Tommaso da Modena
c. 1480–1500, York Minster, screen	1378–1455, Lorenzo Ghiberti 1386–1466, Donatello EARLY RENAISSANCE See *Renaissance and Mannerist Art* in this series

Architecture

Century	France	Germany and Central Europe
13th	Caen, St.-Étienne (choir), c. 1200. Bayeux, 1200–1300. Reims (choir and transept), 1211–41. Le Mans (choir), 1217–54. Amiens (west front and nave), 1220–36. Chartres (transept façades), 1224–60. Saint-Denis (nave), 1231–81. Paris, Sainte-Chapelle, 1243–48. Beauvais (choir), 1247–75 (collapsed in 1284, after which supplementary piers were added) Amiens (south transept), mid-13th century. Troyes, 1250–1506. Reims (façade), c. 1255–90; (rose-window story), 1285. Amiens (choir), 1258–69. Albi, 1282–c. 1480. Toulouse, Jacobin Church, 1230–92. Narbonne, 1272–1319. Paris, Notre-Dame (chapels of the choir ambulatory), 1296–1325. Metz, mid-13th century–1520	Magdeburg (choir), 1209 on; (Bishop's Gallery), 123c Maulbronn (cloisters), 1220–30. Magdeburg (nav and transept), 1235–53. Trier, Liebfrauenkirche, c 1235–53. Marburg, Sankt Elisabeth, 1235–83. Cc logne, cathedral (choir), 1248–1322 Strasbourg (nave begun), 1240; (choir and transep completed), 1250. Naumburg (west choir), c. 1250 Regensburg, begun c. 1250. Altenberg, 1255–1379 Freiburg im Breisgau (nave), 1260 on; (tower), c. 128 –c. 1350. Chorin, 1273–1300. Magdeburg (façade) 1274–1363. Strasbourg (west façade), 1276 on Lübeck, Marienkirche (choir completed), 1291
14th	Rouen, St.-Ouen, 1318 on. Avignon, Palace of the Popes, 1334–42. Reims (west towers), c. 1305–1427	Lübeck, Marienkirche (nave), 1300 on. Vienna (choir) 1304–40. Freiburg im Breisgau (tower octagon), 131c Oppenheim (tracery windows), 1320. Cologne (ded ication of choir), 1322. Chorin, dedicated 1334 Zwettl, 1343 on. Soest, Wiesenkirche, 1343 on Schwäbisch Gmünd, begun c. 1320; hall choir, 135 (by Heinrich Parler III) Prague, cathedral (cornerstone laid by Mathiev d'Arras), 1344; work carried on by Peter Parler, 1353 Ulm, cathedral, 1377–1502. Landshut, Sankt Martin c. 1392–1432. Danzig, Marienkirche, 1343–1502
15th–16th	Rouen, St.-Maclou, 1434–c. 1514. Beaune, Hôtel-Dieu, 1443–51. Mont-Saint-Michel (new choir), 1446 on. Paris, St.-Séverin (apse), 1489–95. Moulins, collegiate church, 1468–1507. Tours (west towers of the cathedral), 1492–1507 Brou, monastery church, 1513–23. Caen, St.-Pierre (choir), 1518–45	Landshut, Heiliggeist Church, 1407–61. Salzburg Franciscan church (choir), c. 1408. Amberg, Sank Martin, 1421–83. Nuremberg, Nassau House (uppe stories), 1422–32. Cologne, Gürzenich Hall, 1437–44 Nuremberg, Sankt Lorenz (choir), 1439–77 Munich, Frauenkirche, begun 1468 Annaberg, Annenkirche, 1499–1520

England	Italy	Elsewhere in Europe
Peterborough (west front), 1201–22. Durham (west towers), completed 1226. Salisbury, 1220–58. Ely (choir), 1234. Lincoln (Gothic parts of west front), . 1250. Durham (east transept), 1242–o. London, Westminster Abbey (choir), 245–60	Casamari, 1203–17. San Martino al Cimino, Viterbo, c. 1210–57. San Galgano, c. 1224–28. Assisi, San Francesco, 1228–53. Pisa, Santa Maria della Spina, 1230–1323. Bologna, San Francesco, 1236–50. Castel del Monte, c. 1240	**Spain:** Tarragona, c. 1120 on. Sigüenza, c. 1150 on. Ávila, c. 1190 on. Burgos, begun 1221. Toledo, begun 1227. Barcelona (choir), begun 1298 **Portugal:** Alcobaça (old Cistercian abbey), 1158–1223 **Low Countries:** Tournai (choir), begun 1242. Utrecht, begun 1254 Cathedrals in Brussels (choir), c. 1225; Ghent (choir), c. 1228; Ypres (St.-Martin), 1221–70 **Sweden:** Linköping, c. 1260. Uppsala, begun 1287
Lincoln (Angel Choir), 1256–1320. Exter (choir), c. 1280–1300. York (nave), 291–c. 1324	Siena, San Francesco, 1250–1326. Siena, cathedral (transept), completed 1259. Arezzo, cathedral, 1277 on. Orvieto, founded 1290. Florence, Santa Croce, begun 1294. Siena, Palazzo Pubblico, begun c. 1297. Florence, Palazzo Vecchio, 1299–1310. Florence, Santa Maria Novella, 1246–1360	
Wells (east choir), enlarged 1300–40. Lincoln (crossing tower), 1307–11. Worcester (nave), 1317–49. Gloucester aisles), 1318–29. Ely (Lady Chapel), 321–49; (wooden vaulting over the rossing), c. 1330. Lichfield (choir), 330–40. Wells (crossing), 1338 on. Exeter (west front), 1346–75. Winchester (nave), begun c. 1350	Venice, Doges' Palace, 1309 on. Venice, Santi Giovanni e Paolo (present structure), begun c. 1333. Florence, campanile (by Giotto), begun 1334	**Low Countries:** Amsterdam, Oude Kerk, 1306–beginning of 16th century. Antwerp, cathedral, begun 1352. Kampen, Sint Nicolaas, begun 1369 **Spain:** Palma de Mallorca, 1306 on. Gerona (choir), begun 1316. Barcelona, Santa Maria del Mar, 1329–83
Gloucester (cloisters), 1351–77. Canterbury (nave), begun c. 1379	Venice, Santa Maria Gloriosa dei Frari, 1330s–1440s. Milan, cathedral, begun before 1386. Bologna San Petronio, begun 1390	
Canterbury (cloister), c. 1400. Oxford, Divinity School, 1430–83. Cambridge, King's College Chapel, 1446–1515. Oxford, cathedral (vaulting), 1480–1500	EARLY RENAISSANCE See *Renaissance and Mannerist Art* in this series	
London, Westminster Abbey, King Henry VII's Chapel, 1503–c. 1512. Windsor Castle, St. George's Chapel, 1473–1528		**Portugal:** Batalha (Royal Cloister), late 15th–early 16th century. Belem, monastery church, 1502–19. Tomar (south portal), 1515 **Spain:** Salamanca, new cathedral, begun 1513. Burgos (crossing tower), 1540–68

Index

Photo credits: Alinari, Florence, p. 76, 77, 78, 79. Dr. Hans H. Hofstätter, Baden-Baden, p. 140 lower, 193, 194, 195, 209, 228, 229, 239, 250. E. Bauer, Bamberg, p. 56, 57, 58, 59, 98 upper, 108, 122, 159, 188, 224, 225, 227. Klaus G. Beyer, Weimar, p. 98 lower. J. Blauel, Munich, p. 162–63. E. Böhm, Mainz, p. 112, 165, 197, 205. Photo Bulloz, Paris, p. 87, 150, 177, 201. Burkhard Verlag, E. Heyer, Essen, p. 82. Dr. H. Busch, Frankfurt am Main, p. 70. S. Ewald, Stralsund, p. 71, 230. R. Friedrich, Berlin, p. 189, 246. Giraudon, Paris, p. 13, 100, 109, 130, 136, 138, 140 upper, 142, 152, 153, 155, 169, 170, 171, 172, 208. Gundermann, Würzburg, p. 221. A. Held, Écublens, p. 92, 124, 125, 126, 127, 128, 129, 132, 143, 149, 181, 206, 207. Holle Verlag, Baden-Baden, p. 23, 38, 72, 99, 100, 102, 104, 131, 145, 173, 176, 190, 211, 232, 233, 240, 241. A. Huck, Strasbourg, p. 214. Dr. M. Hürlimann, Zurich, p. 17, 96 lower. M. Jenni, University Library, Basel, p. 157. A. F. Kersting, London, p. 42, 43, 44, 45, 46, 47, 48, 50, 94, 95. E. E. Kofler, Lucerne, p. 110 upper. Landesbildstelle Württemberg, Stuttgart, p. 121. J. A. Lavaud, Paris, p. 135, 158, 182. Foto Marburg, Marburg, p. 26, 31, 44, 52, 60, 61, 62, 63, 68, 69, 73, 96 upper, 204, 226. E. Meyer, Vienna, p. 160, 216. J. Müller, Soest, p. 51. A. Ohmayer, Rothenburg ob der Tauber, p. 220, 222–23. K. H. Paulmann, Berlin, p. 111, 196, 249. Preiss & Co., Ismaning, p. 178, 180. J. Remmer, Munich, p. 53, 64, 66, 80, 89, 90, 91, 116, 117, 118, 119, 120, 174, 175, 213, 219, 238, 242. Rheinisches Bildarchiv, Cologne, p. 99, 243, 244, 245. O. Rheinländer, Hamburg, p. 103. W. Rösch, Münster, p. 186–87. J. Roubier, Paris, p. 14, 15, 16, 20, 21, 25, 29, 32, 34, 35, 36, 37, 39, 40, 41, 97, 141, 251. Foto Scala, Florence, p. 74, 75, 81, 83, 84, 85, 86, 88, 133, 134, 148. H. Schmidt-Glassner, Stuttgart, p. 113, 114, 115. A. Schimpf, Strasbourg, p. 212. Schmölz & Ullrich KG, Cologne, p. 101, 105. M. Seidel, Mittenwald, p. 18, 27, 28, 30, 33, 106, 123, 147, 161, 164, 198, 199, 200, 210, 218, 231, 234–35, 236–37, 240. Service Archives Photographiques, Paris, p. 22, 107. W. Steinkopf, Berlin, p. 185. K. H. Steppe, Landshut, p. 217. Stober, Freiburg im Breisgau, p. 65, 67, 191. Ulm Travel Bureau, p. 184, 215. ZFA, Düsseldorf, p. 24. The following illustrations were kindly supplied by the museums in which the objects are located: p. 54–55, 110 lower, 144, 146, 151, 154, 156, 166, 167, 179, 183, 192, 202, 203, 242, 252.